Opening up
Titus

DAVID CAMPBELL

DayOne

Opening up
Titus

DAVID CAMPBELL

'The New Testament is not friendly to broad doctrinal tolerance within the Church. Paul's "Pastoral Letters" bristle with instruction that false teachers must be given biting rebukes. The Christian life is founded upon a clear apprehension of the truth.

'At the same time our Saviour Jesus Christ went to the cross with an interest in the life we live "in the present age" (Titus 2:12). He gave himself for us to provide us with zeal for godliness in the here-and-now. David Campbell weaves these and other themes of Titus together with warm and wise pastoral care.'

Walter J Chantry,
Editor, Banner of Truth Magazine

'David Campbell has written a helpful, practical and accessible commentary on Titus. In his warm, insightful and always pastoral exposition, David lucidly opens up Paul's teaching on subjects that have particular relevance to the church today: eldership, false teaching, the importance of sound doctrine, how we are to live as Christian men and as Christian women, the grace of God in salvation, the coming again of our Lord Jesus. The exposition is always faithful to the text and is enhanced by tailpieces to each section providing guidance "For Further Study" and questions "To Think About and Discuss".'

Ian Hamilton,
Pastor of the Cambridge Presbyterian Church, England

First printed 2007

Unless otherwise indicated, Scripture quotations in this publication are from the
Holy Bible: New International Version (NIV), copyright ©1973, 1978, 1984,
International Bible Society.

ISBN 978-1-84625-079-8

9 781846 250798 >

British Library Cataloguing in Publication Data available

Published by Day One Publications
Ryelands Road, Leominster, HR6 8NZ
Telephone 01568 613 740   FAX 01568 611 473

email–sales@dayone.co.uk
web site–www.dayone.co.uk
North American–e-mail-sales@dayonebookstore.com
North American web site–www.dayonebookstore.com

To the congregation of
Geneva Road Evangelical Baptist Church
Darlington, England
With thankfulness to God for our years together
1987-2002

List of Bible abbreviations

THE OLD TESTAMENT		1 Chr.	1 Chronicles	Dan.	Daniel
		2 Chr.	2 Chronicles	Hosea	Hosea
Gen.	Genesis	Ezra	Ezra	Joel	Joel
Exod.	Exodus	Neh.	Nehemiah	Amos	Amos
Lev.	Leviticus	Esth.	Esther	Obad.	Obadiah
Num.	Numbers	Job	Job	Jonah	Jonah
Deut.	Deuteronomy	Ps.	Psalms	Micah	Micah
Josh.	Joshua	Prov.	Proverbs	Nahum	Nahum
Judg.	Judges	Eccles.	Ecclesiastes	Hab.	Habakkuk
Ruth	Ruth	S.of.S.	Song of Solomon	Zeph.	Zephaniah
1 Sam.	1 Samuel	Isa.	Isaiah	Hag.	Haggai
2 Sam.	2 Samuel	Jer.	Jeremiah	Zech.	Zechariah
1 Kings	1 Kings	Lam.	Lamentations	Mal.	Malachi
2 Kings	2 Kings	Ezek.	Ezekiel		

THE NEW TESTAMENT		Gal.	Galatians	Heb.	Hebrews
		Eph.	Ephesians	James	James
Matt.	Matthew	Phil.	Philippians	1 Peter	1 Peter
Mark	Mark	Col.	Colossians	2 Peter	2 Peter
Luke	Luke	1 Thes.	1 Thessalonians	1 John	1 John
John	John	2 Thes.	2 Thessalonians	2 John	2 John
Acts	Acts	1 Tim.	1 Timothy	3 John	3 John
Rom.	Romans	2 Tim.	2 Timothy	Jude	Jude
1 Cor.	1 Corinthians	Titus	Titus	Rev.	Revelation
2 Cor.	2 Corinthians	Philem.	Philemon		

Overview

Frank Houghton's well-known hymn *Facing a task unfinished* challenges us with the needs of those who are as yet unreached with the gospel:

> with none to heed their crying
>
> for life, and love, and light,
>
> unnumbered souls are dying,
>
> and pass into the night.

But it is not just our missionary and evangelistic task that is unfinished. There is also the task that faces each Christian church to put its own house in order. There are needs, responsibilities, and shortcomings, threats to its safety, opportunities to serve the Lord and minister to its members, which each congregation unendingly faces.

The letter to Titus reminds us that there is nothing new about this. There were things 'unfinished' in the first century Cretan church where Titus served and as we read through the letter we discover what they were. They have a familiar ring to them. They are the very things that need to be addressed in our churches today.

But there is so much more to the letter than a mere list of things that needed to be tackled. Under the guidance of the Holy Spirit the Apostle Paul explains why they are to be tackled and how they are to be tackled and by whom. In doing so he gives inspired guidance for churches in all ages as each faces its own unfinished task.

BASED ON THE TIMELINE IN PAUL: APOSTLE OF THE FREE SPIRIT, FF BRUCE, PATERNOSTER PRESS, 1977, P.475

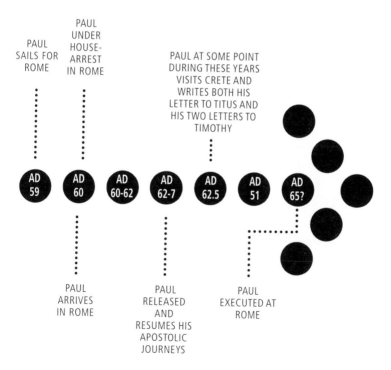

OPENING UP TITUS

Background and Summary

Have you ever got to the end of the book of Acts and said to yourself, 'I wonder what happened next?' Luke really does leave us with a cliff-hanger!

He tells us at length about the apostle Paul coming to Rome as a prisoner and pictures him living in the city under house arrest for two whole years, faithfully evangelising all who come to visit him. And there the book ends! There is nothing about the apostle's trial before Caesar and no word about the outcome. Was he released? Or was it at this time that he was put to death? Acts tantalisingly leaves us wondering.

Most conservative scholars who have pondered the question have concluded that the outcome was favourable to Paul. Caesar released him after his trial, and Paul was able for a time to resume his apostolic travels. That had certainly been his hope and expectation. We learn that from his letter to the Philippians. And there are certain things which would suggest that that hope was realized.

Take, for example, the group of letters that are known in the New Testament as the *Pastorals*—1 and 2 Timothy and Titus. Of the thirteen letters from the pen of the apostle Paul that we have in the New Testament, the Pastorals were the three that were written last, 2 Timothy the last of all. It is argued with considerable plausibility that there are historical details given to us in these letters that do not fit with the story of Paul's life as we have it in the book of Acts. They seem rather to belong to a later period, a period subsequent to his two-year house arrest in the city of Rome.

Assuming, then, that he was released, where did the apostle go? To some extent it is a matter of conjecture. But one place that we do know that he visited—along with his friend and fellow-worker Titus—was the Mediterranean island of Crete. Paul tells us that himself in Titus 1:5.

It is perfectly possible that this was not virgin territory for the gospel. In Acts 2 we learn that there were God-fearing Jews from that island who were present in Jerusalem on the day of Pentecost and who witnessed the amazing scenes of that day. Some of these may well have been converted and returned to Crete with the gospel. What is certain (because the letter to Titus tells us so) is that there were Christian people and Christian churches on the island when Paul eventually left.

> No information has been preserved as to how long Paul was there and why it was that he decided to move on. All we know is that when he left, things were not in an entirely satisfactory condition.

No information has been preserved as to how long Paul was there and why it was that he decided to move on. All we know is that when he left, things were not in an entirely satisfactory condition. There were things that still needed to be done, situations that still needed to be addressed, truths that still needed to be taught. Because of that, when Paul left, Titus remained behind. His task—Titus 1:5—was to 'straighten out what was left unfinished', and in the ensuing letter we are given the details. Both for Titus' own benefit and for the sake of the Christians among whom he was working, Paul felt it necessary to put in writing what exactly needed to be done. Hence, our New Testament letter to Titus.

It is full of tremendous teaching that is just as relevant for the church today as it was for the church in Crete. The qualifications for eldership, the necessity of dealing with false teachers, the importance of sound doctrine, how we are to live as Christian men and as Christian women, the grace of God in salvation, the coming again of our Lord Jesus—all these and more besides are addressed by the apostle. May the study of them be to our spiritual profit!

FOR FURTHER STUDY

1. From a careful reading of all three Pastoral epistles, what details can you discern of Paul's movements and experiences after his release from house arrest in Rome?

TO THINK ABOUT AND DISCUSS

1. If Paul were to write a letter about things that needed to be done, situations that needed to be addressed, truths that needed to be taught in *your* church, what kind of things do you think might be in the letter?

2. Paul lays the responsibility upon Titus to 'straighten out what was left unfinished' in Crete. What about in your own congregation? Who bears the responsibility for addressing the issues you have discussed above? Only the leaders? Or are there responsibilities that devolve upon all?

3. Why are there no apostles like Paul writing such letters to churches today? Are we at a disadvantage with only letters like this one to Titus to consult?

1 From… To…

(1:1-4)

Paul's opening words are not of the 'Hello! How are you?' kind. In a single densely packed sentence he tells us several things about his ministry, introduces us to Titus, and teaches us by example what our prayerful wish should be for our fellow Christians.

When you and I are writing a letter today, it's customary to put our name at the end. Not in Paul's day. Back then you *began* with your name. And that's what Paul does here. He then adds that he is 'a servant of God and an apostle of Jesus Christ'. Most of this first chapter is going to be taken up with an examination of the ministry Paul exercised in that character.

The faith of God's elect

Paul is a servant of God and an apostle of Jesus Christ 'for the faith of God's elect' (v. 1). God has a people in this world whom he has chosen for himself. They are his elect ones—chosen in love before the foundation of the world to be God's own special possession. Here in verse 1 Paul is telling us that his ministry as a servant of God and apostle of Jesus Christ is for their *faith*.

Paul may well be thinking here about his ministry of bringing God's elect *to* faith. That was certainly one of the key aspects of his work as an apostle of Jesus Christ. He preached the gospel both to Jews and Gentiles so that those among them whom God had chosen might come to faith in Jesus Christ.

Paul's concern, however, was not just that faith should begin—vital as that is. He wanted to see their faith increase. On the one hand he knew that a growing faith is one of the great keys to Christian usefulness, happiness, and holiness. On the other hand he knew that God is glorified by a growing faith. Accordingly, it was to the nurture or the increase of their faith that much of his ministry as a servant and apostle was directed. He wanted God's elect to be a people who were strong in their faith, i.e. a people whose faith embraced more and more of divine truth and whose grasp of divine truth was more and more firm.

And that is still one of the great aims of Paul's apostolic ministry. The man himself is of course no longer here in person. He has been in heaven now for the best part of 2,000 years. But his apostolic work goes on. Through the letters that he wrote and which have been incorporated into the New Testament, Paul continues to speak to us as an apostle of Jesus Christ. And he does so for the nurturing of the faith of God's elect.

That is why his letters are so important. That is why with all their difficulties—and there *are* difficulties in Paul's letters!—they need to be read and studied and preached. They are in our Bibles for the nurture and the strengthening of our faith. We need their apostolic ministry if our faith is to be the kind of faith that God wants it to be—a faith that glorifies him and that heightens our Christian usefulness, happiness, and holiness.

And what is true of Paul's letters is equally true of the rest of the Bible. It has all been given for faith. Do you wish to have a faith of increasing depth and breadth? There is no substitute for the reading and study of the word of God as a *whole*. It is to our loss if we neglect any part of it.

The truth that leads to godliness

A second element of Paul's ministry has to do with 'the knowledge of the truth that leads to godliness' (v. 1). One of the many unpleasant features of the days of the prophet Jeremiah was the activity of false prophets. These men professed to be preaching God's message but actually were doing the very reverse. The sin of God's people at that time was exceedingly great, but instead of confronting them with it and calling them to repentance as Jeremiah was doing, these false prophets encouraged the people in their sin. The result was a continuing and deepening ungodliness. The false prophets with their false teaching promoted ungodly behaviour. Not so the apostles of the New Testament! What we hear from *their* lips is rather the truth that leads to godliness.

Prior to our Lord Jesus' return to heaven, he promised his

apostles that when the Spirit came he would guide them into all truth. In their apostolic writings we have the fruit of that promised ministry. In the New Testament letters of Peter, John and Paul, we do not have just the words of men, but rather the very words of the Holy Spirit. He was at work as these men were writing, helping them to express the truth. And here in verse 1 of Titus, Paul tells us what that truth does. It leads to 'godliness'. Unlike the false teaching which promoted ungodliness, Paul's teaching of the truth as an apostle promoted God-centred living. And that was why he taught it!

We see again, therefore, the importance of availing ourselves of Paul's apostolic ministry, of reading and studying the things which he wrote. Such truth if believed and practised will make us Christians of growing godliness. Our lives will be increasingly pleasing to God, increasingly centred on God, increasingly useful to God, and increasingly honouring to God, more and more beautiful with the beauty of God himself.

> What is true of Paul's letters is equally true of the rest of the Bible. It has all been given for faith. Do you wish to have a faith of increasing depth and breadth? There is no substitute for the reading and study of the word of God as a whole.

And again, what was true of Paul's apostolic letters is true of the rest of the New Testament and the whole of the Old Testament as well. God's word is truth—in its entirety—and it has all been given to us for the purpose of promoting godliness. That means that if godliness is the object of our desire, the word of God as a whole must increasingly be studied, known, believed, and lived out by us. We are sanctified through the *truth*.

The hope of eternal life

The third element of Paul's ministry has to do with 'the hope of eternal life' (v. 2). One of the difficulties that we face in this introduction is knowing how some of the parts fit together. Nowhere is that difficulty more acute than when we move from verse 1 to verse 2. In particular there is uncertainty over the connection between the 'hope of eternal life' in verse 2 and the words that precede it.

When we move, however, from the connection of things to the hope of eternal life itself, we move immediately into the realm of the clear and certain. Paul, by the command of God his Saviour (v. 3), preached the hope of eternal life. It was a key element of his ministry as a servant of God and an apostle of Jesus Christ.

To begin with, eternal life is something 'which God, who does not lie, promised before the beginning of time'. Before this world was made, God planned and purposed that certain people, namely, his elect people, would enjoy eternal life.

Life, in its New Testament sense, is a very rich concept indeed. It gathers into one all of the blessings of salvation. All that is ours in Jesus Christ as saved sinners can be summed up in the one glorious word: *life*. At present we do not have this life in its fullest form. There is more to be experienced of it in the future - much more. Paul refers to this when he speaks about the 'hope of eternal life, which God, who does not lie promised before the beginning of time'. He's thinking about the *more* that lies in the future.

'Hope', of course, in everyday speech refers often to something uncertain. You know how often we hope for something that we have no guarantee will happen—especially if it has to do with the weather! In the Bible, however, hope is always something certain. And that is how it is with the hope of eternal life. We can be certain that one day the *more* will be ours—the blessings of salvation in their fullest measure to be enjoyed for ever and ever. For the God who does not lie *promised* eternal life to his elect before this world began. That was his eternal plan and purpose. If, then, we are among God's chosen people we can be certain that this eternal life will be ours.

Ministry Today

In summary, then, Paul in his greeting mentions some of the key elements of his ministry as a servant of God and an apostle of Jesus Christ. And though no person today may rightfully claim to be an apostle of Jesus Christ, these key elements in Paul's ministry remain the key elements in the ministry of every gospel minister. His task, too, is the increase and the nurture of the faith of God's elect, to preach the knowledge of the truth that leads to godliness, and to proclaim the hope of eternal life through faith in Jesus Christ. He cannot do it with apostolic infallibility. But he does have the requisite tools. He has the apostolic gospel. He has the teaching of the apostolic letters and all of the rest of the word of God besides. And with those tools, by the blessing of God, the same great ends that Paul aimed at will be achieved. God's elect will come to faith and enter into possession of the hope of eternal life. Their faith will be nurtured and increased. And as the truth is proclaimed and received into the heart, godly living will be promoted.

> Whatever their religious background, their race, their colour, whatever their sins against God and their crimes against humanity, whatever their social status, they are given the same great welcome when they come in faith to him.

Introducing Titus

Having identified himself as the author and spoken a little of his ministry, Paul now introduces us to the recipient of his letter— 'Titus my true son in our common faith' (v. 4).

Paul is very probably telling us that Titus was one of his converts. Writing to the Corinthians, for example, Paul can say that 'in Christ Jesus I became your father through the gospel' (1 Cor.4.15). As the one who was instrumental in their conversion he could regard himself as their spiritual father. So, too, of his friend Titus.

We do not know very much about Titus. One scholar has described him as the most enigmatic figure in early Christian history. We do know, however—and it illumines very beautifully the statement here about Titus and Paul's 'common faith'—that Titus was a Greek. Paul tells us that explicitly in Galatians 2:3. He was a Gentile, therefore, and Paul of course was a Jew. In terms of background, race, culture, and religious tradition, they had once been poles apart. But now by grace they were *one*—sharers together in a common faith. They had come to believe in the same great Saviour and to participate equally in the same great salvation.

The situation is gloriously the same today. People are often discriminated against on account of their race, their colour, their refugee status, the place where they live, the level of their income, the existence of a criminal record. They are sometimes denied even basic human rights. But no one is ever treated like that when they come as a sinner to the Lord Jesus. Whatever their religious background, their race, their colour, whatever their sins against God and their crimes against humanity, whatever their social status, they are given the same great welcome when they come in faith to *him*. They are given an equal share in the blessings of his grace. They are united to every other believer in the bonds of a common faith. They enjoy the same great salvation and have in Jesus Christ the same great Saviour. There is no discrimination. All believers are members of God's family. All have the Spirit in their hearts. All have the same great inheritance stored up for them in heaven. All have the hope of eternal life.

Grace and Peace

It was common in personal correspondence to bring your greetings to a close with a benediction—an expression of good wishes. *Paul's* benediction is distinctively Christian: 'Grace and peace from God the Father and Christ Jesus our Saviour' (v. 4).

As a Christian, Titus had already known God's *grace*. It was by grace he had been saved. But grace is needed not only at the outset of the Christian life. We need it all our days. It is by grace, for example, that the work of salvation continues. In all its parts, salvation is the fruit of God's unmerited favour. We also need grace in the sense of strength or help— grace to love; grace to forgive; grace to pray; grace to serve the Lord, to endure affliction, to persevere to the end. Knowing that, Paul prayerfully wishes grace for Titus. Shouldn't that be our prayerful wish for others?

Paul also wishes *peace* for Titus. Like every other believer, Titus was vulnerable to anxiety, and Paul would not have him anxious about anything. Instead, he would have him enjoy 'the peace of God that transcends all understanding' (Phil. 4:7) with all the blessing such peace brings. Hence his benediction: 'peace' to you 'from God the Father and Christ Jesus our Saviour.' Shouldn't that be our prayerful wish for others, too?

FOR FURTHER STUDY

1. Read Ephesians 2.14-3.6. What has Christ done to bring once divided peoples to the experience and enjoyment of a common faith? How should this Christ-given oneness be coming to expression in *your* church?

2. In the light of what Paul goes on to say to Titus in Ch2:1-9, what are some of the elements of the godliness to which a knowledge of the truth leads us?

TO THINK ABOUT AND DISCUSS

1. In what ways does faith promote our Christian usefulness, happiness, and holiness? How does it bring glory to God?

2. What kind of blessings does Paul's prayed-for *peace* bring into our Christian lives? How might our experience of this peace be more constant and deep?

2 Profile of a Christian leader

(1:5-9)

A well-written job advert gives you a clear idea of the kind of person who is needed for a particular position. Paul here, under the guidance of the Holy Spirit, gives us something similar. Men are needed for leadership in the church. Here is God's profile of what they are to be.

Greetings over, Paul gets straight down to business. Titus has been left behind on Crete because certain things need to be put in order. The first of these is the appointment of leaders in the churches. Referring to these leaders as *elders*, Paul says, 'the reason that I left you in Crete was that you might straighten out what was left unfinished and appoint elders in every town as I directed you' (v. 5). It would seem that each centre of population had its church. These churches needed leaders. And in verses 6-9, in considerable detail, Paul tells us what kind of men these leaders were to be.

A word about words

Before we examine the profile, we need to glance at Paul's vocabulary. He uses three words to describe these prospective leaders—elder, overseer, and steward.

The *elder* was a very familiar figure among the Jews. There were elders in the synagogue, elders in the Sanhedrin, elders in each town or village. Their role was to preside, to direct, and to govern, and they were appointed on the basis of their wisdom and maturity. The teaching of the New Testament is that *churches* are to have elders as well.

Then there is the word *overseer*, which Paul uses in verse 7. The overseer and the elder are not two distinct persons occupying two distinct offices. They are one and the same. The titles are used interchangeably in the New Testament. An elder is an overseer. And as the title suggests, the overseer has the oversight of a congregation. His duty is to watch over it and take care of it; to protect it and promote its spiritual well-being.

The third title, *steward*, is hidden by the NIV translation of verse 7. A more literal rendering would be, 'an overseer must be blameless as a steward of God'. The steward was the man whom a wealthy master would put in charge of his household or business. It was a position of considerable trust. It required someone who was wise and faithful and trustworthy. And here Paul says that an elder is a steward. He is to manage the affairs of God's house, ensuring that the work of his divine Master gets properly done and caring for his Master's servants.

Elder, overseer, steward—these are the words Paul uses for

the leaders who are to be appointed in our churches. Singly and together they mark the position out as one of considerable responsibility. Evidently a Christian of high calibre is required. That brings us to verses 6-9 and to Paul's Spirit-directed description of the Christian elder.

Clearly, Paul's description is of considerable use to those who already *are* elders. It calls us to self-examination and to seek by the grace of God to be far more the Christian leaders that God intends us to be. The primary concern of these verses, however, is not with *being* the right kind of elders, but with *appointing* them. What kind of men should your church be setting apart for eldership? What kind of men does *God* want in that office? Here in Titus 1 we have a very clear answer!

Summing it all up at the start

The apostle begins with a summary word and later on, in verse 7, repeats it. It is the word *blameless*, and it gathers into one the various elements of the apostle's description.

We do have to be careful here not to impose on this word a meaning that it is not intended to bear. 'This does not of course mean,' writes John Stott, 'that candidates must be flawless or faultless, or we would all be disqualified.'[1] The idea is rather that of being 'above reproach'. Morally and spiritually, the elder is to be exemplary. No one should be able to accuse him of either serious misconduct or a general pattern of inappropriate behaviour. He should have a good reputation among outsiders and within the church as well. And as far as doctrine is concerned, he should be sound.

The elder as a husband

When Paul descends to specifics he begins at home: 'An elder must be blameless, the husband of but one wife'. The basic idea is that of faithfulness. No one is to be made an elder unless he has been faithful to his wife. If he has taken additional wives or has been guilty of adultery, he is disqualified. You can appreciate the importance of this in view of the practices of Paul's day. Immorality was rife. It was common for husbands to sleep with other women. In the community of Jesus Christ, however, a very different standard is to prevail. There is not even to be a hint of sexual immorality (Eph. 5:3). Christian husbands are to be faithful to their wives. And in this, the elders are to take the lead. They are to be patterns of marital purity. Isn't this very much a word for today?

The elder as a father

Paul has more to say about the elder's home life. Not only must he be a faithful husband; he must be a good father, one 'whose children believe and are not open to the charge of being wild and disobedient'. Something needs to be said here before we come to the details. It has to do with the previous point as well. Paul is not saying that a single man, or a widower, or a man who has been divorced on biblical grounds, or a man who has no children, or a man who has only one child cannot be an elder; that in order to be an elder a man must be married with children. What Paul is doing here is focussing on the norm. For the most part, the men in the church who would be eligible for eldership would be married men with children. It is this general situation that he has in mind.

As far as the elder's children are concerned, Paul insists that they 'believe' (NIV). In other translations these children are described, not as *believing*, but as *faithful*—faithful in the sense of submissive or obedient to their father's will. This is a preferable understanding. What is in Paul's mind is not belief but behaviour. He is not saying that an elder's children have to be Christians. But he is insisting that they be under their father's control and 'not open to the charge of being wild and disobedient'. In his first letter to Timothy the apostle makes the same point: 'The overseer…must manage his own family well and see that his children obey him with proper respect' (3:4). Then follows the reason: 'If anyone does not know how to manage his own family, how can he take care of God's church?' (3:5). If a man cannot look after his own household it cannot be expected that he will be able to take care of God's church. Failure in the one area will lead to failure in the other.

> What is needed are men after the pattern of Jesus—humble, gracious, kind, and ready to serve, men who are prepared to spend and be spent for the sake of God's people.

The elder as a Christian man

The matter of home life having been addressed, the apostle turns to the area of personal qualities. Viewing him simply as a Christian man, what is an elder to be like? What follows (vv.

7, 8) are five negatives and six positives.

He must not be 'overbearing'. A church ought never to appoint a self-willed or arrogant man—a man who always wants his own way, who is autocratic and domineering, who likes to lord it over people. What is needed are men after the pattern of Jesus—humble, gracious, kind, and ready to serve, men who are prepared to spend and be spent for the sake of God's people.

He must not be 'quick-tempered'. A prospective elder must be able to handle difficult situations and awkward, irritating people without exploding. Eldership requires patience and the ability to give the 'gentle answer' that 'turns away wrath' (Prov. 15:1). A man who is quick-tempered is not to be appointed.

He must not be 'given to drunkenness'. Literally, he must not be 'given to wine'. Paul was a very balanced man. On the one hand, he could say to Timothy, 'stop drinking only water, and use a little wine because of your stomach and your frequent illnesses' (1 Tim. 5:23). He does not demand that church leaders practise total abstinence. At the same time he insists on the strictest self-control. An overseer must not be given to wine. If a man, therefore, doesn't know when to stop, if he is in the habit of drinking too much, if this is an area where he lacks self-control, he is not to be given the oversight of a Christian assembly.

He must not be 'violent', a man who is ready to have recourse to his fists when he encounters difficulties and conflicts. Tensions do arise in congregational meetings! So too in pastoral counselling sessions and elders' meetings! A man who would be an elder must be able to handle these tensions without becoming violent. He needs to have a peaceable and gentle disposition.

He must not be a man who pursues 'dishonest gain'. There were false teachers in Crete and in verse 11 we learn that one of their characteristics was a pursuit of dishonest gain. They were greedy for money and didn't hesitate to stoop to dishonesty in order to get it. Paul is quite dogmatic on the point: no one who behaves like that is fit for the eldership. An elder must be a man of the strictest integrity as far as money is concerned.

Moving now to the positive, an elder 'must be hospitable'. The word 'hospitable' comes from one which means 'love of strangers'. It is primarily about caring for and welcoming into our homes those who need hospitality or would greatly benefit from it. Examples in our day would be visitors to our congregation, believers who have recently joined us, the lonely, the needy, the singles who are away from their families, etc. Hospitality is a duty that devolves upon us *all*. Paul makes that clear in Romans 12. And in Titus 1 he tells us that it is one of the qualifications for eldership.

He must be a man who 'loves what is good'. There are so many people who love what is bad. An elder, by contrast, must love both things and people deemed by God to be good. Again, he must be 'self-controlled'. A better translation would be 'sober-minded'. The elder is to be a sensible man; a prudent man; not 'given to wild, foolish ideas'[2]. He needs to have sound judgement and be able to exercise wise leadership. He must be 'upright'—living carefully by the standards of God's word in every area of life; 'holy'—seeking day by day to walk closely with God and to please him in everything; and, finally, he must be 'disciplined'. This is the word that is translated 'self-controlled' in Paul's list of the fruits of the Spirit in Galatians 5. In regard to sleeping, eating, the use of time and money, the elder must have mastery of himself. He must not be a slave to his appetites, drives, and desires.

Isn't it striking, as we glance back over these points, how firmly the emphasis falls on qualities rather than gifts; character rather than abilities? Paul really wants us to focus on what a man *is*: 'Be sure of his fidelity to his wife; take note of how he manages his children; examine his personal qualities as a Christian man; be persuaded that in all these things he is blameless. Only then should you make him an elder!' Wouldn't our churches be better cared for if we were at pains to follow these directives?

Last—but definitely not least

In verse 9, Paul brings his list of qualifications to a close by insisting that an elder must be sound in the faith: 'He must hold firmly to the trustworthy message as it has been taught, so that he can encourage others by sound doctrine and refute those who oppose it.' Candidates for the eldership, then, must be examined as to their beliefs. Do they have a good grasp of Christian doctrine? Do they understand the fundamentals of the faith? Are they thoroughly committed to them? In an age like ours where the inspiration of Scripture, justification by faith, penal substitution, God's knowledge of the future, and even the second coming of Christ, are all under attack within evangelicalism, we need to ask—as we value the health of the church—'Do these candidates know and believe the truth?' It is the job of the elders, says Paul, (whether they are full-time in the work or not) to encourage believers with sound doctrine and refute those who oppose it. Unreserved commitment to foundational doctrine is the non-negotiable prerequisite for such a vital ministry.

Gathering it all together, we see how concerned the *Lord* is for his church—for it is he who stands behind the apostle. He knows that his church needs leaders and in the church's highest interests he has told us what kind she needs. The responsibility now is one of implementation. Are you a member of a search committee looking for a full-time elder? Or an eldership that wants to add another man? Or a church member who at the next AGM must vote either yes or no for a particular candidate? Study the profile carefully and resolve, as you do so, that you will settle for nothing less.

FOR FURTHER STUDY

1. In 1Tim. 3:1-7 we have another list of qualifications for the eldership. When you place it alongside the list in Titus, what additional qualifications can you find that help to fill out the picture yet further of what an elder ought to be?

2. Read Acts 20:17-38, Paul's address to the elders of the church in Ephesus. In what ways was Paul himself an example of what an elder should be?

TO THINK ABOUT AND DISCUSS

1. What are some of the benefits that a Christian congregation will enjoy through the oversight of the kind of elders described in Titus 1:5-9?

2. In what ways may a congregation be damaged through neglecting to insist on these qualifications?

3. If your church is considering the appointment of new elders, what specific questions might it be appropriate to ask in the light of these qualifications? (Some examples might be, 'Are the men being considered hospitable to visitors? Are they models of fatherly nurture and discipline in the home?')

3 Dealing with false teachers

(1:10-16)

The church in the twenty-first century has no monopoly on major problems. In the years that followed Pentecost the early church enjoyed remarkable growth and had the privilege of Christ-appointed apostles to guide her. But alongside the blessings were the problems, and of these the most serious was the activity of false teachers. Many parts of New Testament were written to counteract that activity. The passage before us now is one of them.

There are many reasons why churches need the kind of godly leaders that Paul has just been describing, and, doubtless, in urging their appointment he had them all in mind. But it is clear from verses 10-16 that something made their appointment particularly necessary. False teachers were very active in Crete and were posing a serious threat to the believers by the things they were teaching. Thus there is the necessity for elders who would be able to encourage the believers by sound doctrine and refute those who opposed it (v. 9).

In studying the apostle's description of these false teachers it is possible that you may feel the Crete situation to be rather remote from your own. Whatever the problems your church is facing (and every church has problems!), false teaching, you say, isn't one of them. Praise God if that is so! The problem, however, is certainly not remote from the Christian church at large. Just outside her borders, for example, are the cults, those pseudo-Christian groups that pretend to be teaching the true religion of Jesus but whose teaching is horridly subversive of that religion. And within her borders the problem is exceedingly widespread. Many are teaching things that are dangerously at variance with foundational truths and doing immense harm in the process. All of us need to be on our guard against them and to take seriously to heart the apostle's instructions in this passage as to how such people are to be dealt with.

What they were like

In verses 10-16, Paul gives us a detailed description of the Cretan troublemakers—a description that at point after point fits the contemporaries of these men in the Christian church of today.

Beginning with verse 10, we learn that the false teachers were 'rebellious people'—unruly; insubordinate. Here were men who were not prepared to submit to divine authority either in belief or in practice. Their lifestyle and teaching were in open opposition to God's revealed will. Furthermore, they were 'mere talkers' (v. 10). Their teaching was empty and without value. Listening to them brought you no spiritual profit because there was nothing of any real worth in what they were saying. Worse than that, they were 'deceivers' (v. 10). These troublemakers led their hearers astray. Because of the things they were teaching, God's people were embracing doctrines and practices which they imagined to be correct but which most decidedly were not. It all has a modern ring to it, hasn't it?

> The Cretan churches were riddled with false teachers. And, sadly, in the church as a whole, the situation is exactly the same today. Would that such teachers were a rare breed! But they are not.

Then we have some character traits. The false teachers were *greedy*—teaching the things they were teaching 'for the sake of dishonest (or better, 'shameful', 'sordid') gain' (v.11). It wasn't just their doctrine that was bad. Their motive for teaching it was bad as well. They were simply doing it for the money. Isn't that true of some today? Again, they were *typical Cretans*. In verse 12, Paul quotes from a Cretan prophet called Epimenedes who lived several centuries before him. Epimenedes was not very flattering in his assessment of his fellow-islanders: 'Cretans are always liars, evil brutes, lazy gluttons'—a verdict that Paul says was true (v. 13). As a people, that is what the Cretans were like, and we infer from the quotation that that is what the false teachers were like. They were thoroughly representative Cretans.

But Paul isn't finished yet. In addition to all these other things, the false teachers were *corrupt and unbelieving* (v. 15). Whatever their profession may have been, they were not true believers and therefore had never been cleansed by God from the defilement of sin. They were still unclean in mind and in conscience. Finally, from verse 16, we learn that their claim to know God was false. Their lives simply did not match up to such a claim. On the contrary, they were 'detestable, disobedient and unfit for doing anything good.'

It's not a pretty picture that the apostle paints for us, is it? What an affliction for churches to have people like that in their membership! And do you know what is the most disturbing detail of all? It is the word 'many'. There were 'many rebellious people' (v. 10). It would have been bad enough if there had only been a few. But there were *many* of them. The Cretan churches were riddled with false teachers. And, sadly, in the church as a whole, the situation is exactly the same today. Would that such teachers were a rare breed! But they are not.

What they were teaching

In the dark days before the Protestant Reformation of the sixteenth century there was little preaching worthy of the name. Instead of solid biblical exposition, people were subjected to a diet of legendary stories about the saints and their miraculous exploits and experiences. We gather from verse 14 that the first-century Christians in Crete were being treated to similar fare. The false teachers (who it seems were Jews themselves) were teaching 'Jewish myths', which appear to have been fanciful stories about Jewish ancestors. What those stories actually were and where they originally came from need not concern us. It is enough to note that they featured prominently in the teaching the Cretans were receiving.

In addition, the false teachers were teaching man-made laws. Paul refers to this at the end of verse 13 when he speaks about 'the commands of those who reject the truth'. It was a similar problem to the one that Jesus had to contend with. Zealous Jews in his day were binding man-made laws upon the conscience as matters of religious duty. People not infrequently do the very same today.

> It would seem that the Cretan false teachers were taking the same line. They were insisting on abstinence from things that God had said were good, that he himself had given with his blessing, and which could be enjoyed without contracting any moral or religious defilement whatsoever.

It would seem from verse 15 that these man-made laws had to do with religious purity. Paul there insists that 'to the pure all things are pure', meaning that to the *morally* pure—to those who have been genuinely cleansed—all things are religiously clean. Innocent things, in other words, things that God has pronounced good, do not make the true Christian unclean. It would seem that the false teachers were denying this. They were saying that certain innocent things and certain innocent practices were inconsistent with

Christian purity and were calling upon God's people to abstain from them even though God himself had not required it.

In 1 Timothy 4, there are some concrete examples. Paul speaks there about those who 'forbid people to marry and order them to abstain from certain foods, which God created to be received with thanksgiving' (v. 3). It would seem that the Cretan false teachers were taking the same line. They were insisting on abstinence from things that God had said were good, that he himself had given with his blessing, and which could be enjoyed without contracting any moral or religious defilement whatsoever.

What kind of influence they were having

The influence of these men can be summed up in a single word: *harmful*. So much is clear from verse 11, where Paul says to Titus, 'they must be silenced because they are ruining whole households by teaching things they ought not to teach'. The details have not been disclosed. We do not know exactly what Paul means when he talks about whole households being ruined. But the details do not matter. It is enough for us to know that the influence of these men was harmful. Entire families were being devastated through the impact of this false teaching.

It is interesting in this connection to ponder the word 'sound'. Paul gives orders in verse 13 that these men be rebuked 'so that they will be sound in the faith'. The same word is used earlier in verse 9 when the apostle insists that elders must hold firmly to the trustworthy message as it has been taught so that they can encourage others 'by sound doctrine'. And in chapter 2:1, Paul instructs Titus to 'teach what is in accord with sound doctrine'. The word means *healthy*. Sound doctrine is healthy doctrine, doctrine that promotes spiritual health. It is 'truth that leads to godliness' (1:1). Christians are always the better for embracing sound teaching. Not so the teaching of false teachers. Such teaching is always harmful. It is poisonous. In Crete, whole households were being ruined by it. In its most serious forms, false teaching is destructive of our very hopes of salvation. It must never be taken lightly. Rather, it must be something against which we wage war.

What was to be done with them?

Moving from description to remedy, Paul doesn't mince his words: 'They must be silenced' (v. 11). A situation like this was quite intolerable. It could not be allowed to continue. These men were dangerous and must be dealt with. But how was it to be done? In answering that question we notice firstly what Paul says to Titus in verse 13: 'rebuke them sharply'. The false teachers were to be confronted in no uncertain terms with their error—but not by Titus alone. This was to be a *shared* work, and that is evident from verse 9. There we are told that an elder must hold firmly to the trustworthy message so that he can encourage others by sound doctrine 'and refute those who oppose it'. The word translated 'refute' in verse 9 is exactly the same word that is translated 'rebuke' in verse 13. Part of the elders' task is to deal with these troublemakers.

So the picture builds up. There are many churches on the island and Paul wants sound, able, godly men to be appointed as elders in each of them. And part of the reason is that they might unite with Titus in counteracting the influence of these false teachers. 'In the church of God,' says William Hendrickson, 'there is no such thing as "freedom of *misleading* speech." It would be too dangerous.'[1] These false teachers must be silenced. The spiritual safety and wellbeing of God's people demanded it.

What is to be done with them today?

The apostle's unashamedly confrontational approach is the one that is needed today. False teachers dare not be tolerated. They are too dangerous. Their teaching is spiritually harmful. Consequently, it is the unchanging responsibility of church leaders to deal with them when they (or their teaching) begin to threaten the congregation. That is a vital part of shepherding God's flock. And if it means confrontation and sharp rebuke, so be it.

The great difficulty some people have with this is that it seems so unloving. In reality, however, it is not. In fact, the opposite is the case. The unloving thing is to do nothing and let false teachers alone so that they go on spreading their harmful teaching. The loving thing is to follow Paul's directive and rebuke false teachers sharply so that they will be sound in the faith and cease teaching error.

> The unloving thing is to do nothing and let false teachers alone so that they go on spreading their harmful teaching.

Think about the *church as a whole*. The church is harmed by the teaching of such men. It was being harmed in Crete, and it is being harmed across the world today. Love demands, therefore, that Christians do what they can to stop it. Think about *yourself*. If someone started teaching things in your church that were false and harmful, love for you would demand that that teaching be stopped lest you be spiritually harmed by it. Think, too, about the *false teachers*. Part of the reason for rebuking them, as we see in verse 13, is so that they might be 'sound in the faith' and cease to pay attention to those who had corrupted them in the first place (whoever they might have been). A similar point is made in Paul's second letter to Timothy: 'Don't have anything to do with foolish and stupid arguments because you know they produce quarrels. And the Lord's servant must not quarrel...Those who oppose him he must gently instruct' (i.e. instruct with meekness) 'in the hope that God will grant them repentance leading them to a knowledge of the truth' (2:23-25). Isn't it a loving thing to confront false teachers? It may be just the very thing that God will use to bring them to repentance and to the knowledge of the truth.

The need for true teachers

'What was Paul's strategy in the face of spreading error?' asks John Stott. 'It was this: when false teachers increase, we must multiply the number of true teachers.'[2]

That must be the church's strategy today. The great need of the hour is for the kind of sound, able, mature, and godly leaders that Paul has described for us earlier in the chapter— men who are self-controlled, upright, holy, and disciplined; men who hold fast the truth and who are able to encourage others by sound doctrine and refute those who oppose it.

And that being so, we need, among other things, earnestly to petition the Head of the church, the Lord Jesus Christ, for, according to Ephesians 4, such men are his gift. It is he who for the good of his church *gives* such men. In an age of abounding false doctrine, therefore, it is to him that the church needs earnestly to look for the help it so desperately needs.

For further study ▶

FOR FURTHER STUDY

1. In what other New Testament passages are the activities of false teachers addressed? Why should it not be a surprise to us that this was such a widespread problem?

2. In Ephesians 4:11 mention is made of apostles, prophets, evangelists, pastors and teachers. In what different ways has God used such men to counteract false teaching? How does he use them today?

TO THINK ABOUT AND DISCUSS

1. What are some of the harmful effects of false teaching which you have seen? Why do you think God permits false teaching when it does such harm? Can you think of ways in which God has overruled it for good?

2. It was noted earlier that in the face of abounding error we should pray that Christ will give his church godly leaders who can teach sound doctrine. What other steps should the church be taking to address this need?

3. If loving rebuke does not result in errorists becoming sound in the faith and ceasing to teach error, what other options are open to the church as it seeks to silence them? Is it ever legitimate, for example, to invoke the civil authorities? Or is this exclusively a church matter?

4 Teaching for men

(2:1, 2:6-8)

What kind of things should a Christian pastor teach the men of his congregation—the older men and the younger men? What kind of instruction does the Christian pastor need himself? To both these questions Paul gives direct and very helpful answers.

From time to time in his letters, Paul addresses himself to particular *groups*. Writing to the Ephesians, for example, he gives a long series of exhortations to the believers as a whole and then addresses himself to wives, husbands, children, fathers, slaves, and masters in turn. Each group is singled out for specific instruction. The same pattern is followed in the letter to the Colossians.

In Titus 2 the approach is somewhat different. The apostle once again has specific groups in mind—this time older men, older women, younger women, younger men, and slaves— but he doesn't exhort them directly as he does in Ephesians and Colossians. The exhortations are rather to Titus as to what *he* is to teach them. In his own ministry in Crete Titus is to imitate the apostle by singling out special groups for special instruction.

In general, Titus is to teach them 'what is in accord with sound doctrine' (v. 1). We infer from this that doctrine and practice for a Christian are to keep in step with each other. Soundness in the faith is to be accompanied by a lifestyle that harmonizes with it. And Titus's responsibility is to spell out in detail what that means for various groups in the church.

What men who are older are to be

The first group mentioned is the 'older men' (v. 2) and that immediately raises the question of identity. When does one become an older man? We know from ancient Greek literature that the word translated 'older' was used for someone as young as fifty. So maybe we should take fifty as a general rule of thumb. And if you are around that age and consider yourself a borderline case at best, well, you are, by your own admission, at or near the border! You need to heed the apostle's teaching as well!

The first thing that older men are to be is 'temperate'. The idea is that of moderation. The temperate man 'is moderate', says William Hendriksen, 'with respect to the use of wine and in all [his] tastes and habits'[1]. He doesn't go to excess. He is not a slave to his appetites. Whether he is eating, drinking, sleeping, spending money, or engaging in recreation, he keeps a firm hand on his desires and drives.

Again, older men are to be 'worthy of respect'. Some other suggested translations are 'grave', 'reverent', 'dignified', 'serious', or 'respectable'. Paul is not saying that it is inappropriate for older men to have fun. But he does mean that the fun is to be kept within bounds. Older men are not to play the fool. There is to be a seriousness about them that reflects the seriousness of life and the seriousness of the things of God. You who are older men are to conduct yourselves in ways that befit your years. If you do, you will be men of weight, worthy of respect, and a strength to your family and congregation.

Then Paul insists that older men are to be 'self-controlled'. We have encountered this word already in connection with the qualifications for eldership (1:8). There, the NKJV translation is 'sober-minded'. It would be a good translation here. The idea is that of being 'a sensible man; someone known for sound judgment'[2]. And if that is what an older man is, it will certainly be reflected in his life. His speech, his behaviour, the

> Paul is not saying that it is inappropriate for older men to have fun. But he does mean that the fun is to be kept within bounds. Older men are not to play the fool.

decisions that he takes, the counsel that he gives, the responses that he makes to the various situations in life will all bear the stamp of sober-mindedness.

Older men are to be 'sound in faith'. 'Sound', as we have noted before, means 'healthy'. What Paul wants to see in older men is a healthy trust in God. It is to be one of the striking features of their character. Paul himself is an illustration of this. We read in Acts 27 of a violent storm that threatened the lives of all who were on a ship bound for Rome. The men had given up all hope of being saved. But Paul had had a promise that not one would be lost, and he was sure that that promise would be kept. So he stood up in the ship and urged the men to take heart, saying, 'I believe God that it will be just as it was told me' (v. 25). He took God at his word and in so doing displayed a soundness of faith that should characterize every older Christian man (not to mention every other category of Christian!).

Again, older men are to be sound 'in love'. Their love is to be in good health, too. It is not to be allowed to grow cold. Nor is it to be lacking in principle or firmness. If needs be, it is to be *tough* love—love that constrains them to warn, to rebuke, to exhort fellow Christians whom they see to be in spiritual danger. It is to be a love embracive of all, a love that is directed, supremely, to God.

Finally, older men are to be sound 'in endurance'. They are to be examples of perseverance. The older Christian man should not be a waverer—one for whom we feel concern whenever trials come lest they should put him off his stride. Rather, he is to be an example to others of what it means to overcome in the strength of Christ—remaining faithful to him and to his word and to his people through thick and thin, to the very end.

Why?

The question might well be asked, 'Why is it so important that these things be true of older Christian men? Why is Scripture so insistent that chronological maturity—maturity of age—be matched by spiritual maturity?' One very likely reason is that older men in this way will be an example to those who are younger. Commenting on the matter of being 'worthy of respect', for example, John Benton writes, 'there is solidity and commitment to what is right which inspires younger men to secretly say to themselves "I want to be like him"'[3]. Do you older men feel the challenge of that—so to live as to be an example and inspiration to younger Christian men? To provide them with models of godly and mature Christian living that they can follow? To show them what it means to be Christians whose conduct harmonizes with the sound doctrine they have embraced? Surely for the sake of younger Christian men, every older Christian man should seek to be each and all of these things—temperate, worthy of respect, sober-minded, sound in faith, sound in love, and sound in endurance.

Is this your aspiration?

Andrew Bonar was a nineteenth century Scottish preacher. At the beginning of his ministry something was said to him that every Christian man should ponder: 'Remember that very few men and very few ministers keep up to the end the edge that was on their spirit at the first.' In other words, very few Christian men continue to grow and develop and mature as Christians right to the close of their lives. Of many of them it can be said with sad truth that spiritually they are not the men they were in their younger days. Let that not be true of any older Christian who reads these words! Let it rather be your aspiration to exhibit the qualities enjoined on you here and to do so increasingly to the end of your days.

What men who are younger are to be

In verses 3-5 Paul has directives for older and younger women. Leaving those to the next chapter we move on to verse 6 and to Paul's counsel to younger men. Titus is to 'encourage the young men to be self controlled'. The word translated 'self-controlled' here is becoming very familiar to us. It is the same word that is used in chapter 1:8 of prospective elders and in chapter 2:2 of older men. The focus once again is on the mind. Younger men are to be sober-minded. They are to be sensible and clear-headed in their thinking, able to exercise sound judgement.

> Let any younger man who is reading this give himself earnestly to its study! The mind is like a garden. If a garden is not carefully looked after and cultivated, it quickly becomes a wilderness. So it is with a Christian mind. Leave it alone, and it will swiftly become worldly in its thinking.

It is interesting to ponder this in the light of the church situation at the time. These younger men were being exposed to false teaching. Things were being taught in regard to doctrine and duty that were contrary to the will of God. Perhaps that is one of the reasons why we have this directive about the mind. In the face of so much that was false these young men urgently needed to have the qualities of mind and judgement that would keep them from being led astray.

There is a wider aspect to this as well. Sober-mindedness, as we saw in connection with older men, is a whole-of-life thing. It has a positive and wholesome impact upon our speech, our behaviour, the decisions that we make in life, the counsel that we give to others, the ways in which we respond to the various situations of life. Its value cannot be over-estimated

How then is it to be obtained? The plain answer is— through the Bible. In the Bible we have the mind of Christ and of God; clear directives from heaven as to how we are to live and what we are to believe. Let any younger man who is reading this give himself earnestly to its study! The mind is like a garden. If a garden is not carefully looked after and cultivated, it quickly becomes a wilderness. So it is with a Christian mind. Leave it alone, and it will swiftly become worldly in its thinking. If then you would be sober-minded— a sensible, prudent Christian marked by sound judgement— steep your mind in the Word of God!

What men who are leaders are to be

Verses 7 and 8 are specifically for Titus himself: 'In everything set them an example by doing what is good. In your teaching show integrity, seriousness and soundness of speech that cannot be condemned, so that those who oppose you may be ashamed because they have nothing bad to say about us.' Paul is clearly addressing Titus in his character as a Christian leader. His words are applicable to all who occupy a similar position within the Christian church today.

Conduct

They tell us first of all what a leader is to be in his conduct, namely, an example: 'In everything set them an example by doing what is good.' By 'them' Paul may well mean *all* the groups that he has been mentioning—older men, older women, younger women, younger men, perhaps even the false teachers of whom he has been speaking in chapter one. To the congregation as a whole, Titus is to set an example by doing what is good. His life is to be a pattern of good works for all to see and imitate.

But let us think specifically about the younger men. One of the abiding challenges that face Christian leaders is to set an example to the younger men of the assembly in regard to what is good. We are to be a model to them. They should be able to look at our lives and see how young Christian men should live. Isn't that a challenge? Whether it be as husbands, fathers, sons, workers, or as leaders within the assembly, we are to be a pattern of good works that younger men of the assembly can see and imitate. In our relationships with the opposite sex, in our attitudes toward money and possessions, in our commitment to the Lord Jesus Christ and his church— in all these things and many more we are to set an example of what is good.

Teaching

We learn secondly from Paul's words what Christian leaders are to be in their teaching: 'In your teaching show integrity, seriousness and soundness of speech that cannot be condemned'. John Stott sums it up neatly in terms of motive, manner, and matter. The Christian teacher is to be characterized by purity of motive (unlike the false teachers who peddled their doctrines for gain), seriousness of manner ('People will not take serious subjects seriously', says Dr. Stott, 'unless there is a due seriousness in the preacher's manner and delivery'4), and soundness of matter (doctrine that is pure and healthy).

He is to be a man of integrity who with appropriate seriousness gives sound teaching to his congregation.

If that is the kind of teacher he is, his congregation, by God's blessing, will benefit greatly. But notice how Paul ends his exhortation—not with the believers in Crete but with Titus's opponents: 'set...an example by doing what is good', and 'show integrity, seriousness, and soundness of speech so that those who oppose you may be ashamed because they have nothing bad to say about us'. We are back to the false teachers and any other opponents that Titus may have had. Paul is anxious that none of them should have just grounds for charging Titus with wrongdoing. The reputation and effectiveness of the gospel were at stake. If Titus was to fail in regard to his conduct and ministry as a

> One of the abiding challenges that face Christian leaders is to set an example to the younger men of the assembly in regard to what is good. We are to be a model to them. They should be able to look at our lives and see how young Christian men should live.

Christian teacher, his opponents would be swift to make capital out of it. And Titus must be at pains to prevent that.

It is an exhortation that every Christian leader needs to take to heart. Serious failures in conduct and ministry not only do harm to the people of God, but they damage the reputation of the gospel and hinder its effectiveness among unbelievers. Paul could say to hypocritical Jews in Romans 2, 'God's name is blasphemed among the Gentiles because of you' (v. 24). May God help leaders in the church so to live and minister that the same will never be said of them.

FOR FURTHER STUDY

1. An example was given from the life of Paul of what it means to be sound in faith. Can you think of any biblical examples of soundness in love and in endurance?

2. Paul, perhaps surprisingly, mentions only sober-mindedness as the quality to be enjoined upon young men (though in Paul's insistence that Titus be an example of good conduct to younger men, it is implied that they should follow that example). What other counsel does Scripture explicitly direct to young men?

TO THINK ABOUT AND DISCUSS

1. Why do you think it is—as Bonar's friend put it—that 'very few men and very few ministers keep up to the end the edge that was on their spirit at the first'? What practical steps can older men take to prevent this happening?

2. What concrete examples can you think of that illustrate the impact of sober-mindedness upon the life of a younger Christian man?

3. In what ways do the serious failures of church leaders in conduct and ministry damage the reputation of the gospel and hinder its effectiveness among unbelievers? Think of any high-profile media cases that illustrate this point. How might such episodes of failure have been prevented from taking place?

5 Teaching for women

(2:3-5)

If you are an older Christian woman, there is a certain pattern of behaviour that is expected of you. There is also a particular work that the Lord has for you to do. Your experience of life puts you in a unique position to help younger Christian women be the wives, mothers, and homemakers that the Lord intends them to be. Here in verses 3-5 Paul provides the details.

Sandwiched between the teaching that is to be given to older men (v. 2) and that which is to be given to younger men (v. 6) is instruction for older and younger women.

What women who are older are to be

There are certain things that Titus is to teach older women to be, namely, 'reverent in the way that they live, not to be slanderers or addicted to much wine, but to teach what is good' (v. 3).

Here there is the same preliminary question that there was with the older men. What age of woman does Paul have in mind? It appears that we can at least say this: older women are those whose children are now grown up. The raising-a-family stage of life is behind them. One of their duties—as we shall see later—is to train the younger women to love their children (v. 4). The assumption is that they have had practical experience of this themselves and are now able to use their experience to help the younger women.

The first thing that older women are to be is 'reverent in the way that they live'. The word translated 'reverent' occurs only here in the New Testament. The basic idea is that of 'conduct appropriate to a temple' and suggests that older women are to behave in ways befitting those who are servants of God. Others may please themselves in the way that they live and recognize no higher authority than their own wills. Older Christian women are to be different. It is to be apparent from the way they live that their lives are dedicated to God.

Again, older women are 'not to be slanderers'. In the use of their tongues they are to exercise strict self-control. It was as common then as it is today to engage in malicious gossip; to spread rumours about people; to say unkind things about them and damage their reputation. No such speech is to be heard on the lips of an older Christian woman.

Older women are 'not to be...addicted to much wine'. Drinking to excess seems to have been a common practice among the older women of that time and is certainly not unknown today! It is to have no place, however, among *Christian* women. They may be lonely; they may be facing difficulties; they may be tempted by neighbours and friends. Nevertheless, as Christian women, their duty is clear: they are not to be addicted—literally *enslaved*—to much wine.

Finally—and here Paul moves from the negative to the positive—older women are 'to teach what is good'. The things that they have learned in the course of their Christian lives are to be shared with others, particularly, as we learn from verses 4 and 5, with the younger women. Older women, then, are not to be self-absorbed; they are not just to be thinking about themselves. They are to be concerned about others, particularly the younger generation. And in various different ways—formally and informally, by word and by example—they are to teach them what is good so they too might live lives that are pleasing to God and a blessing to others.

What women who are younger are to be

In verses 4 and 5 Paul specifies the good things that the older women are to teach the younger. They are to train them 'to love their husbands and children, to be self-controlled and pure, to be busy at home, to be kind, and to be subject to their husbands, so that no one will malign the word of God.' These words serve a dual function. They not only help the older women to understand their responsibility toward the younger; they help the younger to understand what kind of Christian women they themselves are to be.

The mention of 'husbands and children' indicates that Paul is dealing here with the norm; with what is usually the case. A young woman will marry and have children. We know from 1 Corinthians 7 that Paul had a very high view of singleness, particularly because of the special opportunity it provides for Christian service. Nevertheless, he recognized that most young women would become wives and mothers. It is such that he has in mind in these instructions.

Younger women are first of all to be trained 'to love their husbands'. Marital love is something that Paul talks about elsewhere—briefly in Colossians, at greater length in Ephesians. In both passages he addresses husbands. A Christian husband is to love his wife and is to do so as Christ loved the church and gave himself up for her. Here in Titus the picture is rounded out. The love of a husband is to be matched by the love of a wife.

Does it sound surprising that younger women are to be *trained* to love their husbands? Prior to her wedding a young woman may imagine that nothing could be easier than to love her husband. But Paul knew better. There may be things about a husband that make loving him difficult. Or it may be that the difficulty in loving him lies with the young wife herself. Here is where the older, more experienced Christian woman can help with appropriate counsel.

> There may be things about a husband that make loving him difficult. Or it may be that the difficulty in loving him lies with the young wife herself. Here is where the older, more experienced Christian woman can help with appropriate counsel.

So, too, in regard to children. Young mothers are to be trained 'to love their…children'. It is not love to so indulge our children that they always get their own way. Nor is it love to refuse to discipline them. Showing love means making wise decisions about appropriate behaviour and disciplining when there is disobedience. Young mothers may need help in this, and older women should be there to help them.

> It is not love to so indulge our children that they always get their own way. Nor is it love to refuse to discipline them. Showing love means making wise decisions about appropriate behaviour and disciplining when there is disobedience.

Young women are to be 'self-controlled'—just as younger men (v. 6), older men (v. 2), and elders (1:8) are to be. The focus once again is on the mind; on having a sensible outlook on life that will filter down into sensible behaviour.

Again, younger women are to be 'pure'. Marriage does not exempt a woman from sexual temptation. She may find herself attracted to another man. She may even fall into adultery. Knowing all that, Paul insists on purity. A young Christian woman is to be faithful to her husband—even if things should be difficult in the marriage.

Younger women are to be 'busy at home'. Literally, they are to be home workers. That does not mean that married women should never have a job outside the home. It does mean that for a young wife, her home is to have the priority. Old-fashioned as it may sound, it is the thing that is to come first—not her career. A wife has a responsibility before God to ensure that her home is properly managed. She is so to take care of things and order things at home that it is a place where her husband and children are happy to be.

Another thing that younger women are to be is 'kind'. Paul may have been especially thinking here about kindness in the home. If a Christian woman was wealthy she might well have servants or slaves. If so, her duty was to be kind to them and not harsh. Then there is the matter of hospitality—opening our homes to visitors and to people who are in need and sharing time and food with them. We learn from chapter 1:8 that this is one of the duties of an elder. In Romans 12:13, however, Paul urges *all* believers to be hospitable. It is an important way of showing Christian kindness. And it is just such kindness that is to characterize younger Christian women.

Younger Christian women are to be 'subject to their husbands'. It is the clear teaching of the New Testament that just as Christ is the head of the church, so God has constituted the husband the head of his wife. Paul states that clearly in both Ephesians and Colossians. The husband's role is that of a leader within the home, and it is the duty of his wife to accept and follow his leadership. This in no way implies that a husband is superior to his wife. Nor does it ever give him the right to tyrannize, abuse, or bully. A husband's leadership in the home is to be characterized by the self-giving love that is seen in Christ's relationship to the church. But he is to *lead*. And just as the church is subject to Christ and accepts his leadership, so a wife is to be subject to her husband.

The importance of teaching

It is an interesting expectation that Paul has here. He doesn't say 'Titus, you need to take the younger women aside and teach them these things.' This is a responsibility of the older women. Granted, in the preaching of this letter in church, or in a male-led Bible study on it in the home, a man is going to be involved in teaching these things to any young women who are present. Nevertheless, the teaching responsibility is placed here on the older women. Their greater age, wisdom, maturity, knowledge, and experience give them special competence in this area.

How it is actually to be done is not specified. Much of it will doubtless take place informally. A young wife has a question, perhaps, and approaches an older Christian for counsel. Or the older Christian sensitively takes the opportunity to give counsel when she sees that it would be helpful. A great deal can be done in the context of conversation and through the cultivation of Christian friendship. At a more formal level, the instruction can be given through Bible studies or at a ladies conference. But whether formally or informally, the important thing is that it gets done!

This is especially important in the context of a society that has so largely thrown off God's good and righteous standards. For example, take the young woman who has grown up in a home marked by behaviour the very opposite of what Paul is pleading for here. Where is she to see and how is she to learn what it really means to be a Christian wife and mother? It is the responsibility of older Christian women—formally and informally, by word and by example—to teach her.

The importance of heeding

Some of the things Paul is insisting on here are hated and ridiculed in today's society—especially those that have to do with marriage and the home. There are professing Christians who thoroughly dislike them as well. But they are not mere matters of first century culture that can be dismissed as out of date. We can see that from the opening words of the chapter. Titus is to 'teach what is in accord with sound doctrine', instructing the Cretan Christians how to live in a way that harmonizes with the truth. And in his description of what a young woman should be, Paul is simply spelling out in detail what that means.

The importance of heeding this instruction is pressed home in the final words of verse 5: 'so that no one will malign the word of God'. What is at stake here is the reputation of our Christianity, our gospel, our Saviour. It is absolutely true that God's way is always the best way. The young woman who heeds these instructions will find it to be in her own, her husband's, and her children's highest interests. But the thing that is uppermost in Paul's mind is the public image of our faith. Where there is a failure to adopt this godly lifestyle, people will make it an excuse for maligning the word of God. They will hold the gospel responsible for a Christian woman's misconduct and as a consequence will treat it with contempt. 'If young mothers', writes William Hendriksen, 'professing to be Christians, should manifest lack of love for their husbands and for their children, lack of self control, of purity, domesticity, kindness, and submissiveness, they would cause the message of salvation to be evil spoken of by outsiders.'[1]

On the other hand, if young women take heed to these matters and refuse to let opinions that are antagonistic to the word of God determine their behaviour, then by God's blessing, that word will be honoured. For they will be showing how wholesome is its impact and how attractive are the lives and families it produces.

FOR FURTHER STUDY

1. In three other New Testament passages—Ephesians 5, Colossians 3, 1 Peter 3—the subject of a wife's submission to her husband is addressed. What—in addition to the duty itself—is to be learned from these passages about this important subject?

2. The book of Proverbs has some very helpful material on practical ways in which parents are to love their children. What are some of its instructions?

TO THINK ABOUT AND DISCUSS

1. Discuss some concrete ways in which the responsibility of older women to teach younger women can be fulfilled. How could you implement some of these ideas in your church?

2. What are some of the difficulties that a young woman can face when it comes to loving her husband and children? What counsel should an older woman give in response?

3. What does it mean in practical terms for a woman to be subject to her husband? What kinds of things make that submissiveness hard or easy?

4. What are some of the key areas where non-Christian thinking conflicts with the teaching of these verses? How can Christians protect themselves against such thinking?

5. In what ways is the word of God in danger of being maligned today through failure to follow Paul's directives?

6. What can a young woman who is single learn from this passage?

6 Words for workers

(2:9, 10)

You are a Christian in the workplace and asking the question: 'How would God have me conduct myself as a Christian worker?' In this section originally addressed to Christian *slaves* Paul lays down principles that are just as applicable to twenty-first century employment situations as they were to the work situations faced by slaves in the first century.

The Roman world of Paul's day was full of slaves. It is estimated that were somewhere in the region of fifty million of them—including a third of the inhabitants of Rome. People became slaves because they were taken as prisoners of war, or as a punishment for certain crimes, or because of debt, or through kidnapping, or through being sold into slavery by parents. Some sold themselves into slavery, and many were born slaves. They worked as domestic servants, farm labourers, clerks, craftsmen, teachers, soldiers, and managers. Some were even doctors! They could be treated harshly—Roman law did not forbid that—but were often treated kindly. They might be permitted to buy their freedom and apparently were often set free by their master's last will.

Today we look upon slavery with feelings of abhorrence. It appals us to think of people owning other people and depriving them of the freedom we enjoy. Surprisingly, however, the New Testament itself does not condemn slavery. It does condemn the activities of the slave-trader (e.g. 1 Tim. 1:10). But we look in vain for condemnation of the practice of actually having slaves. 'Probably the main reason,' writes John Stott, 'is that slavery was deeply embedded in the structures of Graeco-Roman society...In consequence, to dismantle slavery all at once would have brought about the collapse of society. Any signs of a slave revolt were put down with ruthless brutality...At the same time Paul enunciated principles which undermined the very concept of slavery and led inexorably to its abolition.'[1]

Where the issue of slavery *is* explicitly addressed in the New Testament the focus is on the responsibilities that Christian masters and slaves have toward each other. In two of his letters, for example, Paul has certain things to say to Christian *masters*. In Colossians 4:1 he commands them to provide their slaves with what is right and fair, 'because you know that you also have a Master in heaven'. Similarly in Ephesians 6 he instructs masters not to threaten their slaves, 'since you know that he who is both their Master and yours is in heaven, and there is no favouritism with him' (v. 9). Masters, then, are not free to do with their slaves whatever they please. They are to regulate their conduct by the fact that they themselves have a Master in heaven and treat their slaves with fairness, justice, and kindness. In Titus 2, however, the focus is not on the master-slave relationship but on the slave-master relationship. How are Christian slaves to behave in relation to their masters? Paul tells us explicitly in verses 9 and 10.

In approaching these verses, our principal concern is with the bearing of Paul's teaching on ourselves. What does a passage about slaves have to say to readers who are free? To be specific, does it have anything to say to us about how we should conduct ourselves at work? In answering that question, the differences between our situation and that of the slaves on Crete need to be acknowledged. An employee-employer relationship is one which we voluntarily enter into and which an employee may terminate when he wishes. Nevertheless, the principles of conduct laid down here by Paul do apply to us. Titus is to teach the workers of his day how they are to conduct themselves as *workers*. And we may learn from what is said here how to conduct ourselves as workers in our own day.

The HOW

The primary focus of these verses is on *how* Christian slaves are to conduct themselves in relation to their masters. The Apostle makes five points.

Slaves are to be subject to their masters in everything (v. 9). The duty of submission is emphasized in several other passages. In Ephesians 6:5 Paul writes, 'Slaves, obey your earthly masters with respect and fear, and with sincerity of heart, just as you would obey Christ.' Again, in Colossians

3:22 he says, 'Slaves, obey your earthly masters in everything; and do it not only when their eye is on you to win their favour but with sincerity of heart and reverence for the Lord.' Peter takes up the subject as well: 'Slaves, submit yourselves to your masters with all respect, not only to those who are good and considerate, but also to those who are harsh' (1 Peter 2:18).

Lying back of these commands is a recognition that masters have a legitimate authority over their slaves and that their authority is not to be rebelled against. Just as people in general are to be subject to rulers (Titus 3.1) so slaves are to be subject to their masters. Paul's addition 'in everything' is not of course to be understood in an absolute sense. If a master ordered his slave to steal or kill or lie, he was under *no* obligation to obey. His duty in such circumstances was to obey his Master in heaven. But where there was no clash between the will of God and the will of his earthly master, the Christian slave was to be subject to his master in everything, doing whatever work was required of him.

> An employee-employer relationship is one which we voluntarily enter into and which an employee may terminate when he wishes. Nevertheless, the principles of conduct laid down here by Paul do apply to us.

In regard to employment, the same limitations exist as in the case of slavery. An employer's authority is not absolute. If, for example, you are instructed to do something dishonest or untruthful, you are under no obligation to obey because what you are being required to do is what God has forbidden. But where there is no conflict between God and your superior, you, as a Christian worker, are to do exactly what is expected of you—even if it is something you would much rather not do.

The basic problem here is our sinful human hearts. 'There are few things more distasteful to modern man than subjection to authority and the demand for obedience to authority'[2] It is not something that is liked. Nevertheless, it is something required of us as Christian workers.

Slaves are to try to please their masters (v. 9). They are to endeavour to give them satisfaction. This involves being conscientious and hardworking. If a slave is lazy, or does his work carelessly and half-heartedly, he will certainly not please his master. Does God require anything less of those who are in voluntary, paid employment? It ought to be a constant aim of Christian employees to give their employer satisfaction. And that means exactly the same as it did in the realm of first century slavery. Lazy workers or workers who do their work carelessly and half-heartedly will certainly not please their superior. We need to be conscientious and hardworking.

Slaves are not to talk back to their masters (v. 9). Here we come to the spirit in which the work is to be done. A slave receives his orders and is not happy with what he is told to do. So he makes a surly remark. He grumbles and complains. He may go on and do the work well enough, but he has done it in a resentful spirit and with resentful words. 'That', says Paul, 'is wrong. Teach slaves *not* to talk back to their masters'.

Regardless of how common and acceptable it may be in the eyes of many, it is forbidden to the Christian slave. He is to do his work in a right spirit, willingly fulfilling the tasks that his master has assigned him.

The standard is surely no lower for workers in employment situations. Christians are to be characterized by self-control in the use of their tongues. And that means that we are not to talk back to the person who is giving us our instructions. To be cheeky, rude, surly, and complaining when told to do something is forbidden to us. God requires that we not only *do* the work that we are set but that we do it in a right spirit—willingly and without grumbling.

Slaves are not to steal from their masters (v. 10). Many slaves were in positions of trust. The opportunities were there to take things that did not belong to them and either keep or sell them. And human nature being what it is, many of them would have done it. Here again, however, the will of God is plain. Christian slaves are to be honest and *not* to steal from their masters. Regardless of what others are doing they are to submit to the authority of the eighth commandment and have nothing in their pockets or their homes that they have not been given or earned.

The legitimacy of applying this to the workplace today is utterly beyond dispute. The authority of the eighth commandment is unchanged. It remains the will of God that we do not steal. Interestingly, the word translated 'steal' may be translated 'pilfer'. What is in mind here is not massive fraud but petty thieving. Office stationery, little bits and pieces, things that will not be missed, the claim for more expenses than have been incurred—those are the kinds of things the text is targeting. When I worked as a student in a factory bakery, I would sometimes see men going off with a couple of bread rolls in their pocket. And of course many people see no harm in it. But the Christian worker is to be scrupulously honest. He or she is not to steal anything. If it does not belong to us, if we have no right to it, if we do not have our employer's permission for taking it, it is to be left severely alone.

Slaves are to show that they can be fully trusted (v. 10).

Here the great biblical example is Joseph. He was a slave in the house of Potiphar, an Egyptian official, and the Lord so blessed and helped him that Potiphar eventually put him in charge of his household and entrusted everything he owned to his care. 'With Joseph in charge', it is recorded, 'Potiphar did not concern himself with anything except the food he ate' (Gen. 39:6). Joseph was utterly trustworthy.

> The Christian worker is to be scrupulously honest. He or she is not to steal anything. If it does not belong to us, if we have no right to it, if we do not have our employer's permission for taking it, it is to be left severely alone

Paul is anxious that Christian slaves should bear a similar character. However they may differ from one another in terms of abilities and responsibilities they should all show that they are to be fully trusted. Their master should be able to rely upon them to be honest and conscientious workers.

And that is the will of God for *all* workers. No less a standard is demanded of Christians today. Whatever the position we occupy—from cleaners to senior managers—we should show ourselves to be fully trustworthy. There should be no doubt as to our honesty and commitment to doing our job well.

The 'why'

Having explained at length how Christian slaves (and by extension today's Christian workers) are to conduct themselves, Paul concludes this brief section with a reason: 'so that in every way they will make the teaching about God our Saviour attractive' (v. 10).

It is most certainly the case that the people with and for whom we work need *teaching*. Employers, managers, fellow workers—they need to hear about God our Saviour and what he has done in Christ to save sinners. And as God gives us opportunities we are to endeavour to share the gospel with them.

But it is not to end there. Non-Christians in the workplace need more than just the truth. They need to see the outworking of it in our lives. They need to see the pleasant and lovely difference that Jesus has made to us. And that is why we need to take these instructions to heart and, by God's, seek grace to put them into practice. It is by just such conduct that we make the teaching about God our Saviour attractive.

Granted, the submission, the effort to give satisfaction, the willing spirit, the honesty and trustworthiness required of us as workers will not in themselves secure the salvation of a colleague or boss. Christians may set the best of examples and yet meet with hostility on account of their faith. Nevertheless, the way in which we do our jobs as Christians may be just the thing that God will use to attract people to himself. And, therefore, we need to feel the challenge of this passage. It is only too true that by the way we work we can bring discredit upon the gospel; we can make the teaching about God our Saviour repugnant. Let it be our constant concern to do the very opposite.

FOR FURTHER STUDY

1 In the quotation from John Stott in the introduction to this chapter it was said that 'Paul enunciated principles which undermined the very concept of slavery and led inexorably to its abolition.' Do you agree? If so, what are some of those principles? Are there other biblical principles in addition to those of Paul's?

2 From parallel passages that deal with slave-master relationships and other parts of Scripture what are some of the additional principles that we ought to apply as we seek to conduct ourselves in the workplace as Christians ought?

TO THINK ABOUT AND DISCUSS

1. What are some of the areas in modern employment situations where a conflict may arise between the will of an employer and the will of God? In what ways are these best addressed?

2. What practical steps can you take to ensure that you are giving satisfaction to your employer? What counsel would you give to Christians whose superiors are unreasonably hard to please?

3. How can you keep a surly and complaining spirit in check and instead do your work willingly?

4. In what concrete ways can you show yourself to be a worker who is wholly trustworthy? Suggest at least three ways in which you could concentrate your efforts in this regard.

7 Living in the light of his coming

(2:11-15)

One day this present age will have run its course. When it has, our great God and Saviour, Jesus Christ, will come again and introduce a whole new order of things. But how are to we to live in the meantime, as we wait for this great event? The grace of God in salvation and the self-giving of Christ on Calvary together point us to the answer.

The New Testament repeatedly traces our experience of salvation to its roots in the grace of God. In 2 Timothy, for example, Paul reminds us that 'God…has saved us and called us to a holy life—not because of anything we have done but because of his own purpose and *grace*' (1:9). Then there is the succinct declaration of Ephesians 2, made and then repeated—'it is by *grace* you have been saved' (vv. 5, 8). And now here in Titus 2:11 we are told that 'the *grace of God* that brings salvation has appeared to all men'. It is God's unmerited favour to which the whole experience goes back.

It is very likely that the word order of verse 11 as it is in the NIV should be changed. A better translation might read like this: 'For the grace of God has appeared that brings salvation to all men', that is, to all kinds and classes of people. God's grace knows no barriers. It recognizes no distinctions. It brings salvation to young and old, rich and poor, male and female, slave and free, Jew and Gentile alike.

What grace does

This grace of God is a powerful force in our lives as believers. As Paul puts it in verse 12, 'it teaches us to say "No" to ungodliness and worldly passions, and to live self-controlled, upright and godly lives in this present age'. Grace not only brings about initial change; it enables us thereafter to live truly Christian lives.

As it does so, we may become very Christlike indeed. Nevertheless, to the end of our days, we will carry around with us hearts that are wicked. And because of that, there is a constant possibility of sinning. We can be guilty of 'ungodliness'. We can yield to 'worldly passions', i.e. to the sinful desires that are all too prevalent in a world in rebellion against God.

That being so, we can appreciate the value of God's saving grace. What does it do? It 'teaches us to say "No" to ungodliness and worldly passions'. Left to ourselves we would be no match for sin. We would fall before it like the skittles in a bowling alley. Apart from the mighty influence of God's grace in our lives, we would find ourselves constantly saying 'Yes' instead of 'No' and yielding to all kinds of temptations. It is by God's grace alone that we are able to renounce such behaviour and instead 'live self-controlled, upright, and godly lives in this present age.'

It has often been said that these three words—self-controlled, upright, and godly—each look in a different direction. Self-control has reference to ourselves; uprightness to our fellow men; and godliness to God. There is, in other words, nothing unbalanced about the life grace enables us to live. There is an all-roundedness about it. The aim of divine grace is to make us Christians who in every area of life—man-ward, self-ward, and God-ward—are well-pleasing to God.

> These three words—self-controlled, upright, and godly—each look in a different direction. Self-control has reference to ourselves; uprightness to our fellow men; and godliness to God. There is, in other words, nothing unbalanced about the life grace enables us to live.

That being so, our clear duty is to co-operate with this grace and not resist it. It is taking us in the direction of a life in which ungodliness and worldly passions have no place; a life in which self-control, uprightness, and godliness hold absolute sway. And we are steadily to follow its leadings, adopting daily the godly lifestyle—already outlined in part in verses 2-10—that it is prompting and empowering us to adopt.

Until he comes...

As we read on into verse 13, it is apparent that Paul has a particular reason for this emphasis on God's grace. He speaks there of 'the blessed hope—the glorious appearing of our great God and Saviour, Jesus Christ'. It is something yet in the future. The 'present age' to which he refers at the end of verse 12 has not yet run its course. How are we to live in the meantime, as we wait for Christ's return? The grace of God in salvation—teaching us to renounce sin and to live lives that are in every way pleasing to God—supplies us with our answer.

Something certain

It is time now to move on to the glorious appearing itself, noticing, to begin with, that Paul describes it as our 'hope'. Normally when *we* use the word 'hope' the reference is to something *un*certain. We hope that we're going to get the job we have applied for—but of course we cannot be sure. We hope that we shall be able to visit again next year—but there is no guarantee that we will be able. Hope is not the sort of word we use when we are speaking about something certain!

But in the Bible it is different. We noted that when looking at the hope of eternal life in chapter 1:2. Hope is repeatedly used for blessings that will one day be ours. We do not have them yet. They still lie in the future. But they are promised to us and are therefore sure. And that is very much the case with the glorious appearing of our Saviour. It is a subject of explicit and repeated promise. He is coming back! That's why Paul can speak about it here as our 'hope'.

Something wonderful

He further describes it as our '*blessed* hope'. How will things be when our hope is realized? Immeasurably the better! It is often said that for believers, 'the best is yet to be'. It is absolutely true. Though the future may have many a dark shadow over it and there may be many hard things to bear, it still remains true that the best is yet to be. And that is because of our '*blessed* hope'. The hope of the second coming is a hope whose realization will bring wonderful blessing into our lives. Here are two examples.

There is the blessing of *resurrection*: 'Our citizenship is in heaven,' says Paul to the Philippians. 'And we eagerly await a Saviour from there, the Lord Jesus Christ, who, by the power that enables him to bring everything under his control, will transform our lowly bodies so that they will be like his glorious body' (Phil. 3:20, 21).

And there is the blessing of *comfort*: 'Now the dwelling of God is with men, and he will live with them. They will be his people, and God himself will be with them and be their God. He will wipe every tear from their eyes. There will be no more death or mourning or crying or pain, for the old order of things has passed away' (Rev. 21:3, 4).

A Divine Saviour?

It has been argued that when Paul speaks about the appearing of our 'great God and Saviour, Jesus Christ', he is actually referring to *two* persons—'the great God', i.e. our Father, and 'our Saviour Jesus Christ'. Nevertheless, there are grammatical and theological reasons for giving the preference—as the NIV does—to a *one* person reference. What we have here in this verse is an ascription of deity to Christ. He is our 'great God and Saviour'.

At the level of Greek grammar, for example, the verse is constructed in such a way that this is the most natural way to translate it. The facts are as follows: There are two nouns in the same case—'God' and 'Saviour'. The first one has the definite article 'the' and the other does not. And they are joined by the conjunction 'and'. When you come across such a construction in Greek the reference is to *one* person unless there is a strong reason to the contrary.

In this case there is not. To quote from J.M. Boice, 'Since Paul is writing of the second coming and sudden appearance of Jesus both words must refer to *him*, for it is not God the Father who is going to appear suddenly but rather "our great God and Saviour" who is Jesus'[1]. The Saviour, therefore, for whose appearing we are waiting, is a *divine* Saviour.

Jesus' Self-Giving

In verse 14 the Apostle reminds us of what this divine Saviour did for us when he appeared the first time: he 'gave himself for us to redeem us from all wickedness and to purify for himself a people that are his very own, eager to do what is good'. It is a picture of remarkable condescension and overflowing love. For we know what this self-giving involved. It involved the death of the cross. To every aspect of its sufferings—from the betrayal, the arrest, the trial, to the crucifixion itself with its shame and God-forsakenness—he freely 'gave himself'. And the reason? It was for our redemption and purification.

Redemption

Imagine you were back in the first century—the slave-world of Paul's day. There are a number of slaves in your congregation. They have heard the gospel, believed in Jesus, and are now saved. Among them is one whose situation is particularly distressing. He has a very cruel master and though becoming a Christian has made this slave a better worker, his master, if anything, is even more cruel to him. So you decide to try and secure his freedom. You offer to buy the man and his master agrees to sell him. What have you done for this slave? You have redeemed him! By the payment of a price you have secured his freedom from the cruel tyranny to which he was subject.

> It was necessary that we first be purified. We needed to be cleansed from our sin as well as delivered from its enslaving power if we were to be Jesus' special, good-doing people. And that was only possible through Jesus' sacrificial self-giving.

It is that kind of transaction that helps us to understand Jesus' death. He gave himself for us to 'redeem us'. He paid the price of his own life to obtain freedom for us. And Paul tells us what that freedom was from: 'all wickedness', literally, all *lawlessness*. Think of the life you were living before your conversion. As far as the law of the land is concerned you may have been a law-abiding citizen. You didn't steal cars, burgle houses, or do drugs. But as far as the law of God is concerned, it was an entirely different matter. At point after point your life was out of line with God's law. It was full of things that that law both forbids and condemns. Lawless! And it was precisely in order to set us *free* from such lawlessness that Jesus gave himself for us.

Purification

His purpose in dying for us, however, went beyond this. He 'gave himself for us,' says Paul, 'to purify for himself a people that are his very own, eager to do what is good.' To be eager to do what is good is to be the very opposite of being lawless. A person who is eager to do *good*—in the New Testament sense of that term—is eager to please his Saviour and to do what he would have him to do. He wants to obey, to serve, to worship. And it was to have just such a people for himself that Jesus died. It was necessary that we first be purified. We needed to be cleansed from our sin as well as delivered from its enslaving power if we were to be Jesus' special, good-doing people. And that was only possible through Jesus' sacrificial self-giving.

Until he comes…

We naturally ask, 'Why is Paul telling us this?' Primarily, to answer a very basic question: 'How are we to live in the meantime?' This present age continues. Christ has still to appear. How are to conduct ourselves as we wait for the fulfilment of the blessed hope? Part of the answer has already been given in what has been said about the grace of God in salvation. And now in Christ's self-giving on Calvary we have another part of it. Since Christ has given himself for us to redeem and purify us, it is for each of us to fall in with that purpose and never seek to thwart it.

In practical terms it means that lawlessness in every form is to be shunned. It means being eager to do what is good. Specifically, in the context of Paul's concerns in chapter 2, it means following the directives that he has given for the various different groups. We are not to think for one moment that these are merely Paul's opinions. The truth is far otherwise. Christ *died* that we might live such lives. And it is our unchanging obligation to fall in with that purpose—to be what he has purposed we should be; to do what he has purposed we should do—until he comes.

Final directives

The Apostle ends this section by again emphasizing Titus's responsibility in regard to the various different groups he is to instruct: 'These, then, are the things you should teach' (v. 15). Right at the beginning of the chapter Titus is exhorted to 'teach what is in accord with sound doctrine' (v. 1). Now the exhortation is repeated. These details of Christian duty, with the impulses to obedience from the grace of God and the self-giving of Christ, are to be the subject of clear and careful instruction.

Paul then adds, 'Encourage and rebuke with all authority' (v. 15). Titus is not only to tell the Cretans how they are to live. He is to exhort and encourage them to carry his instructions out and to rebuke them for any failure to do so. And he is to do so 'with all authority'. These instructions on godly living are ultimately Christ's, conveyed to the Cretans through an apostle whom Christ has authorized to speak on his behalf. They have the backing of heaven and are to be delivered and received accordingly.

Finally, Paul says 'Do not let anyone despise you' (v. 15). Titus is to command the people's respect as he labours among them as a teacher. How? By being an example of the godly lifestyle that he is preaching to others. In a similar exhortation to Timothy, Paul writes, 'Don't let anyone look down on you because you are young, but set an example for the believers in speech, in life, in love, in faith, in purity' (1 Tim. 4:12). Titus is to follow a similar path: 'In everything set them an example by doing what is good' (Titus 2:7).

There is much here for teachers and preachers today. We are certainly to teach the doctrines of the word of God. Doctrines are foundational. But we are also to teach the duties that correspond to those doctrines and to clearly set before our hearers what godly living looks like. We are to do so with exhortation and rebuke, urging obedience and reproving sin, and all with the authority of Christ, if it is truly Christ's directives that we are giving. And we are to be at pains to model this godly living ourselves. If we are to command our hearers' respect and gain for our message the welcome that it ought to receive, we must exemplify that message in our own lives.

For further study ▶

FOR FURTHER STUDY

1. Two aspects of the blessedness that will be ours at the second coming were mentioned in this chapter—resurrection and comfort. What are some of the other blessings that the Scriptures connect with Jesus' return? What impact are these anticipated blessings intended to have on us in the present?

2. Titus 2.13 is one of the few places in the New Testament where Jesus is explicitly called GOD. What are some of the other places? Why do you think—since the deity of Christ is so important—that the New Testament authors so infrequently speak of him in this way? In what other ways is this grand doctrine established?

TO THINK ABOUT AND DISCUSS

1. In what different ways does grace teach or instruct us to say 'No' to sin and to live godly lives instead? Pinpoint at least three areas in a person's life where these principles need to be kept in mind and applied.

2. Paul speaks at the beginning of verse 13 of believers 'waiting' for or 'looking' for the appearing of Christ. What do you think that means in practical terms? What difference does such a conscious expectation of Christ's return make to a believer's life? How do we sustain it in view of the very long time (from our perspective) that he has tarried in heaven?

8 The Christian in the world

(3:1, 2)

Though we cross at this point into a new chapter, the apostle's concern remains the same as it has been, namely, the promoting of godly living. In the previous chapter the focus has been on various groups in the church—older men, older women, younger women, etc.—and the conduct appropriate to each. Here in this section his focus is on believers as a whole and the manner in which they are to conduct themselves in the world.

It should come as no surprise when Christians suffer persecution. It is exactly what Jesus led us to expect. Speaking to his disciples before his death, for example, he could say to them, 'If you were of the world, the world would love you as its own. Yet because you are not of the world, but I chose you out of the world, therefore the world hates you' (John 15.19).

Obviously by 'the world' Jesus doesn't mean 'the planet'—

the world of trees, plants, mountains, lakes, and fields. He is speaking about the unconverted, that is, human beings in rebellion against God. *They* are the world. It was for this reason that he could say to his disciples 'you are not *of* the world'. They had crossed a line. They belonged now to a separate grouping, quite distinct from their rebellious fellow humans. That is why they were hated. It is why Jesus' disciples are hated still.

But while believers are not *of* the world they are nevertheless *in* the world. The Lord does not take his people to heaven the moment they are born again. It is his will that for a time at least we remain here—notwithstanding the world's hostility to us. He has important work to do in us in sanctifying grace. And he has important work for us to do for him.

To help and encourage us as we remain in this world, certain provisions have been made for us. In answer to our Saviour's prayer, for example, we enjoy divine protection: 'My prayer is not that you take them out of the world but that you protect them from the evil one' (John 17:15). We enjoy, too, the divine presence. 'I will not leave you as orphans', said Jesus to his disciples; 'I will come to you' (John 14:18)—a promise fulfilled in the presence of the Holy Spirit.

Furthermore, we have divine guidance as to how we are to conduct ourselves in the world. Titus 3:1 and 2 is a sample of that guidance. Titus is to remind the believers 'to be subject to rulers and authorities, to be obedient, to be ready to do whatever is good, to slander no one, to be peaceable and considerate, and to show true humility toward all men'. Here is clear teaching on how we are to live as Christians as we continue on in the world.

In the course of these instructions a transition takes place. The Apostle begins with the Christian in relation to the governing authorities and ends with our duty to *all* men. It is not easy to determine at what point in the series he moves from the one to the other. There is, in fact, some overlap. But the various instructions are clear in themselves and we shall take them one by one.

Rulers and Authorities

'Remind the people,' says Paul, 'to be subject to rulers and authorities' (v. 1). There was once a proud king of Babylon called Nebuchadnezzar who had some painful lessons to learn. This was one of them: 'The Most High is sovereign over the kingdoms of men and gives them to anyone he wishes' (Dan.4:32). It is God who puts people or parties in positions of authority. The Apostle Paul makes a similar point in the first verse of Romans 13: 'There is no authority except that which God has established. The authorities that exist have been established by God'.

In the same verse Paul tells us what this means for us in terms of duty. It is, in fact, his opening note: 'Everyone must submit himself to the governing authorities'. Since God has put them in power we are to be in subjection to them. And here in Titus 3.1 the same point is made. Titus is to remind the believers that they are to be 'subject to rulers and authorities'.

Obedience

Reading the first verse literally, we learn that 'to rulers [and] authorities' we are 'to be subject, to be obedient'. The latter word is explanatory of the former. Being subject to governing authorities involves being *obedient* to them.

Scholars have pointed out that this was much needed counsel for the Cretans. Their island was in the hands of the Romans, and by all accounts the Cretans were very restless under their yoke. Hence the apostolic counsel. It had clearly been given before, for Titus is to *remind* them of it. 'You may wish that you were free from Roman rule, but for the time being God has placed you under it. It is your duty to submit to it. Do what the authorities tell you. Fulfil your obligations.'

> We are to recognize the hand of God in the appointment of those who govern us, and we are to be obedient to them. We are to be law-abiding citizens.

And we of course are to do the same. We are to recognize the hand of God in the appointment of those who govern us, and we are to be obedient to them. We are to be law-abiding citizens. We may be very unhappy with certain government actions and may pray that in his mercy God will one day give us better leaders. But for his own purposes he has placed them over us and it is our duty as Christians to live in conformity with their laws.

Questions must be asked, however, about the *extent* of our submission. Must we *always* do what the ruling powers say? Or is there a legitimate place for civil disobedience? In answering this, the Bible indicates that there are limits to a ruler's authority and that when those limits are transgressed, it is right to disobey. Some incidents from Bible history will illustrate this.

In the Exodus 1 we learn that when the Israelites were multiplying in Egypt, Pharaoh became afraid of their growing power. So he commanded the Hebrew midwives to kill every new-born baby boy. 'The midwives, however, feared God and did not do what the king of Egypt told them; they let the boys live' (v. 17).

Then there are the well-known examples from the book of Daniel. In chapter 3, Shadrach, Meshach, and Abednego choose to be thrown into a fiery furnace rather than worship the golden image that their king had commanded them to worship. And in chapter 6, Daniel, at the risk of his life, defies the king's decree that for thirty days no one should pray to anyone other than him.

As a final example—this time from the New Testament— we have the refusal of the apostles to stop preaching about Jesus when ordered to do so by the Jewish authorities. Their principle (and it applies to all of the incidents above) is succinctly stated for us in Acts 5:29: 'We must obey God rather than men.' It does sometimes happen that the will of an earthly ruler conflicts with the will of God. And when that happens, it is *God* whom we are to obey. His authority is supreme.

For many of the early Christians this meant death. They were to pay Caesar divine honours by calling him 'Lord'. That was the imperial command. But they refused because they knew that if they were to do this they would be giving to Caesar what was due to Jesus alone. And in many instances they paid for their disobedience with their lives.

It may well be that in days to come we will find it necessary to act on the apostles' principle ourselves. May God give us courage if such days should come! Where, however, there is no clash between the will of God and the will of the government, we are to be loyal and obedient subjects. We are to pay our taxes, observe the speed limits, implement health and safety regulations, fasten our seatbelts, and in all other respects keep on the right side of the law.

Doing good

Titus is to remind the believers further 'to be ready to do whatever is good' (v. 1). 'It is not enough,' writes John Stott, 'for Christians to be law-abiding (so far as our consciences permit us); we are to be public-spirited as well'[1]—ready to what is good. If, for example, a state of emergency was declared on account of some disaster, it would be our duty as citizens to do what we could to assist. Or if there was just cause for our country to go to war, public-spiritedness would demand that we assist the war effort by serving in the military or helping in some capacity on the home-front. Caring for the environment is another instance in which Christians should do good.

> Where ... there is no clash between the will of God and the will of the government, we are to be loyal and obedient subjects.

It is very likely, however, that Paul has more in mind here than simply our duty as citizens. Readiness to do whatever is good is surely to characterize us as neighbours, friends, family members, colleagues, fellow students, and Christian brothers. It is something for which believers should be notable in every relation of life. We are to show in all kinds of practical ways that we are genuinely concerned for people; that we have their best interests at heart; that if it is possible to be of help to them, we are willing to help.

Our speech

According to verse 2, Titus is to remind the believers 'to slander no one'. The reference is to insulting and abusive language. William Hendriksen translates it 'revile'[2]. 'It imports,' says Patrick Fairbairn, 'more than to speak evil in the ordinary sense; it is to act the part of a reviler or slanderer; and when used of conduct from one man to another, always betrays the exercise of a very bitter and malignant spirit.'[3]

The apostle's directive could not be clearer. No such abusing and insulting language is to be heard on our lips. We may feel it necessary to criticize a certain politician, for example, or a fellow believer, or a colleague at work, or a family member. And the criticism may be justified. But we must be exceedingly careful about the way in which we express it and be at pains to avoid the kind of language that Paul is condemning here.

Our great example in this respect is our Lord Jesus, 'who, when he was reviled, did not revile in return' (1 Peter 2:23, NKJV). 'Bless those who persecute you,' writes Paul in Romans 12; 'bless and do not curse' (v. 14). People may be insulting and abusive in their language to us but by God's grace our language to them is to be altogether different.

Peaceable and considerate

When we are called in verse 2 to be 'peaceable' Paul is using a word that can be translated 'not contentious', or 'not quarrelsome'. The AV renders it 'to be no brawlers', i.e. people who are ready to resort to violence in difficult situations. It is an aspect of self-control. Tensions may be running high in the office, the home, or the church meeting but we are not to make matters worst by exploding in uncontrollable anger. Instead we are to be 'considerate', i.e. gracious, conciliatory, peace-makers. A believer is to be anxious to heal rather than to deepen wounds; to preserve peace rather than to destroy it.

Humility

Paul concludes his instructions for Christians in the world by exhorting us 'to show true humility toward all men'. In Jesus' beatitudes in his Sermon on the Mount, he pronounced the meek to be blessed (Matt. 5:5). It is the same word that is used here. We are to show all *meekness*. In our relationships with others we are to be gentle, humble, considerate, and courteous—not arrogant, abrasive, domineering, and proud.

The closing two words are important: 'all men'. In Colossians 3 meekness is something that is required of us in our relationships within the church (v. 12). Here the reference is broadened to include everyone. It is not just among our fellow Christian that this grace is to be displayed. There is to be a gentleness, humility, and courteousness about our manner *whomever* we are with.

Our witness

When Paul was writing the second chapter of this letter, he had a very evident concern for the witness of Christians in the world. We see that in verses 5, 8, and 10. It is in every way likely that the same concern lies behind his instructions in chapter 3:1 and 2. It is not enough for Christians to *say* the right things—telling others about Jesus and his love. Our lives are of critical importance, too. People need to see a consistency between the salvation that we profess to have received and the way we live in the world. And in these reminders to be subject to rulers and authorities, to be ready to do whatever is good etc., we have clear pointers as to the direction in which we must go as we seek to reduce Paul's concern to practice.

For further study ▶

FOR FURTHER STUDY

1. What are some of the reasons given in Scripture why Christians are not taken straight to heaven when they are born again?

2. What other biblical examples are there of a legitimate refusal to obey those in authority?

TO THINK ABOUT AND DISCUSS

1. What examples can you think of outside the Scriptures of civil disobedience by Christians? Are you able to defend these actions on the same grounds as the apostles defended theirs? In what kinds of acts of civil disobedience would you be able in good conscience to join non-Christians? In which would you not be able to join them?

2. One area where Christians are evidently reluctant to obey the authorities is in the matter of observing the speed limit. Why is this? Is observing the speed limit to be considered optional?

3. In what areas do you foresee it to be possible that civil government may pass laws that Christians will be constrained in conscience to disobey?

4. What examples of public-spiritedness can you add to the ones already given? How important do you think it is that Christians be good citizens in this respect?

5. What are some of the practical difficulties that you face at work, at school or college, or among non-Christian family members in being peaceable, considerate, and meek? How might they best be overcome?

6. Can you think of an example of a non-Christian being drawn toward Christ through a Christian taking Paul's instructions in this passage seriously?

9 God's saving work

(3:3-8)

Five times in the Pastoral Epistles—1 Tim. 1:15; 3:1; 4:8, 9; 2 Tim. 2:11-13; Titus 3:4-8—Paul gives us what he calls a 'trustworthy' or 'faithful' saying. These appear to have been well known among the early Christians, and each receives Paul's apostolic endorsement. Here in Titus 3:4-8 we have the last and longest of them—a saying that celebrates God's saving work in his people's lives.

If you were to make a list of New Testament passages that illustrate how greatly God in salvation has blessed his people, you would certainly want to include *this* one and might well put it near the top. Paul tells us here that notwithstanding our great sinfulness (v. 3) we have been the objects of God's kindness, love, mercy, and grace (vv. 4, 5, 7). And the fruit of it is rebirth and renewal by the Holy Spirit, justification, and the hope of eternal life (vv. 5-7).

Before we come to the details there is an important

question we need to ask. Why does Paul say these things at this point in his letter? The answer is found in verse 8 where Paul writes to Titus, 'I want you to stress these things, so that those who have trusted in God may be careful to devote themselves to doing what is good.' There is a lifestyle that he wants believers to embrace, one that is characterized by good works. And it is in order to motivate us to do those good works that he reminds us of God's saving work in our lives. The passage fits in, therefore, with what is evidently one of Paul's major concerns in the letter as a whole, namely, the promoting of godly living.

The great things God has given us

The three words in verse 5 that the NIV gives us twice over, 'he saved us', are the key words in the passage. They tell us what this 'trustworthy saying' is principally about—God's saving work in our lives. But what does it all mean? What does God actually *do* when he saves us? Paul identifies three things that are given to us.

A new beginning

Many would love to make fresh start. They are not happy with the way their lives have gone, with the things they have experienced and done. If only they could begin again! In a very real way when God *saves* us he gives us that very thing. Paul speaks in verse 5 about 'rebirth and renewal by the Holy Spirit'. It is the language of new beginning. From this point onward a whole new life begins—a life of faith, penitence, love, and obedience.

This is no exaggeration. There is nothing superficial about

the Spirit's renewing activity at the outset of our Christian lives. One writer has described it as an 'all-pervasive moral transformation changing the whole man in heart, disposition, inclination, desire, motive, interest, ambition and purpose'[1]. The Scriptures bear that out. It is what God promised through the prophet Ezekiel when he said, 'A new heart...will I give you and a new spirit will I put within you' (Ezek. 36:26). And further, 'I will put my Spirit in you and move you to follow my decrees and be careful to keep my laws' (Ezek. 36:27). We are radically *changed* when the Spirit renews us. The whole of our nature is affected for good. And the change inevitably shows itself in the way that we live.

Of course, as every Christian knows, to renew is not to perfect. We still carry around with us a heart that is sinful, and, because of that to devote ourselves to doing what is good (v. 8) can sometimes be a struggle. But through the Spirit a transformation has begun. And that transformation always makes itself visible in the adoption of a lifestyle that is pleasing to God.

A new standing

According to verse 7, God in saving us has not only renewed us. He has also 'justified' us 'by his grace'. It is the language of a new standing or legal status.

Imagine you are a defendant in a court of law—the man or woman accused. The evidence has all been sifted; the jury has finished its deliberations; and now the critical moment for the verdict to be announced has come. Guilty or not guilty? 'Not guilty!'

Whenever such a thing happens the defendant, to use

Paul's word in verse 7, has been *justified*. It is a legal word and means to find and declare that in the eyes of the law the person accused is innocent and therefore free to leave the court.

It is this amazing thing that God does when he saves sinners. He justifies them. In spite of all the sins of which they are justly chargeable he is now able to regard and treat them as righteous in his sight. He forgives their sins, frees them from the condemnation they deserve, and makes them heirs of eternal life.

From other passages of Scripture—most notably Paul's letters to the Romans and the Galatians—we learn in detail how God can do such a thing righteously. We learn that it is wholly on account of Christ. It is because of his perfectly obedient life and his sacrificial death that God can justly forgive and treat as righteous those who believe in him.

Here in Titus, however, it is simply the *fact* of our justification that is stressed. We have a new standing! Right up to the moment God saved us we stood guilty and condemned. But now our standing in his sight is altogether different. Through Christ our sins have all been pardoned. A perfect righteousness has been credited to our account. God can justly regard and treat us now as if we had perfectly kept his law. And he both does and will!

A new future

It is said of the Old Testament character Enoch that 'he walked with God' (Gen. 5.24). The same may be said of every Christian. In giving us a new beginning and a new standing, God has brought us into a very close relationship with himself. We have peace with him because he has justified us (Rom.5.1), and we have a heart for him because he has renewed us. The fruit of it is that we *walk* with him.

It is the language of intimacy, friendship, companionship. We are no longer separated from God as we were before our sins were dealt with. There has been reconciliation and re-union. We now go through life together, because he is with us all the time. As we do so we *talk* with each other. We talk to God in prayer; he talks with us through the Scriptures. Furthermore, as we journey on in his company we try to serve him, do his will, and bring glory to his name. That is Christian *life* for us!

> It is said of the Old Testament character Enoch that 'he walked with God' (Gen. 5.24). The same may be said of every Christian.

And the great thing is that this life with God is going to go on for ever and ever. It is eternal. Having been 'justified by his grace', verse 7, we have 'become heirs having the hope of eternal life'. What a contrast this new future presents to the one that we had before God saved us! That was as dark as can be imagined. We were on our way to hell. But now we have the prospect of eternal life. We have become heirs to it. We are going to walk with God *always*— in the unending enjoyment of his friendship and love.

In seeking to attract sinners to Christ, preachers will often speak about the privileges that Christians enjoy. They have every warrant to do so. In saving us God has given us a new beginning, a new standing, and a new future. Our privileges are great indeed!

What moves God to give these things

There is more to this trustworthy saying than an enumeration of God's good gifts to us. We also learn what moves God to give them.

Firstly, and negatively, it is 'not because of righteous things' that we have done (v. 5). Think about what we sometimes do with young children. Their toys are scattered all over the room, and we tell them to pick them up and tidy them away. We know of course that they will not be able to do it perfectly. But we want them to make the attempt. And when they have done it we are happy to do the rest.

> They make an effort to clean up their lives and keep God's commandments in the hope that he will deem that to be enough. But God does not save us in that way.

There are many who seem to think that that is how *God* acts. They make an effort to clean up their lives and keep God's commandments in the hope that he will deem that to be enough. But God does not save us in that way. He does not take note of what we do, feel pleased with us, and then reward us by doing the rest. It is 'not because of righteous things' that we have done!

This is a note that the New Testament strikes frequently. In Ephesians 2, for example, Paul reminds his readers that 'by grace you have been saved…not by works, so that no one can boast' (vv. 8, 9). In Romans 3 the same apostle writes, 'we maintain that a man is justified by faith apart from observing the law' (v. 28). The point is made again in Galatians where Paul states that 'a man is not justified by observing the law, but by faith in Jesus Christ' (2:16). And in a personal note in Philippians Paul says that his desire is 'to gain Christ and be found in him, not having a righteousness of my own that comes from the law, but that which is through faith in Christ' (3:9). The good things we have been given have not in any way been earned by us.

What was it then that *did* move God to give them? Four words stand out as we read through the passage—kindness, love, mercy, and grace. It was 'when the *kindness and* love of God our Saviour appeared' that he saved us (v. 4). It was 'not because of righteous things we had done, but because of his *mercy*' (v. 5). It was 'by his *grace*' that he justified us (v. 7).

These words of course have their own distinct meanings. Mercy, for example, takes account of our *helplessness* and points us to God's pitying, compassionate heart. Grace has reference to our *undeservingness* and again speaks of God's pitying, compassionate heart. What a thoroughly wretched state we were in! We were 'foolish, disobedient, deceived and enslaved by all kinds of passions and pleasures. We lived in malice and envy, being hated and hating one another' (v. 3). Nevertheless we were the objects of God's love. And it was that that moved him to *save* us.

A godly lifestyle

There is an important principle that we see illustrated in various parts of the New Testament: great blessings place us under great obligations. Take, for instance, Romans 12.1: 'Therefore, I urge, you brothers, in view of God's mercy, to offer your bodies as living sacrifices, holy and pleasing to God.' For eleven chapters Paul has been writing about God's mercy to us in salvation. And now, at the beginning of chapter 12, he turns to the obligation this mercy has placed us under and urges us to offer ourselves to God.

We have another example at the beginning of Philippians 2: 'If you have any encouragement from being united to Christ, if any comfort from his love, if any fellowship with the Spirit, if any tenderness and compassion, then make my joy complete by being like-minded, having the same love, being one in spirit and purpose' (vv. 1, 2). Paul is reminding us of our blessings—our union with Christ, our comfort from his love, our fellowship with the Spirit, our experience of God's tenderness and compassion—and is indicating what our response to these blessings should be. We should be like-minded; we should have the same love; we should be one in spirit and purpose.

Then there is our present passage. Why dwell at such length on the great things God has done in his love and kindness? The answer, as we noted at the beginning, is found in verse 8: 'I want you to stress these things, so that those who have trusted in God may be careful to devote themselves to good works'. God's mercy calls us to a lifestyle characterized by good works. It obliges us to devotedly do what is good. And it is in order to motivate us to fulfil this obligation that Paul has spoken of the things that he has.

Doing good is a very broad-ranging thing. It ultimately takes in the whole will of God for us. It means being all that God wants us to be whether as husbands or wives, parents or children, brothers and sisters in the Lord, neighbours, colleagues, employers, workers, citizens, or friends. The apostle himself has given us some of the details in the course of chapter 2. And our abiding concern should be to take these details and out of thankfulness to God for what he has done for us to seek in a devoted way to fulfil them.

For further study ▶

FOR FURTHER STUDY

1. In his first letter John has a great deal to say about the new beginning we have experienced through rebirth and renewal by the Holy Spirit. Read through the letter, noting the relevant verses, and see from them just how radical a change in us the Spirit has wrought. What, according to John, are the elements of that change?

2. With many contemporary challenges to the doctrine of justification by faith, it is important to be clear about what justification means. Look up Deuteronomy 25:1 and Proverbs 17:15 where justification is clearly a legal term and has to with a judicial pronouncement. How, in the light of these texts can God righteously justify the ungodly (Rom. 4:5)?

TO THINK ABOUT AND DISCUSS

1. In the light of the radical change that takes place at the beginning of the Christian life, what are we to think about (and perhaps say to) the person who professes to have been born again and yet gives no evidence of being any different from a non-Christian?

2. What is it about our fallen human nature that makes it necessary for the New Testament so repeatedly to emphasize that our salvation is by grace and not by works?

3. Paul seeks to motivate us to good works by reminding us of God's grace in salvation. In what other ways does the New Testament encourage us to do good works? What especially motivates *you*?

4. Make a list of ways in which you think you could make more of an impact in your life through the practice of good works

10 Final instructions

(3:9-15)

Over the centuries of her existence, the church has both been plagued with men who have caused division and blessed with men who have done great good. In this closing section of Paul's letter we encounter the two types. Helpful instruction is given as to how we should deal with the first and how we should encourage the second.

Titus's ministry on Crete was shortly going to end. A replacement for him would be arriving in the near future—either Artemis or Tychicus (v. 12)—and it was Paul's wish that Titus then do his best to join him at Nicopolis (on the Adriatic coast of modern Greece), where he was planning to spend the winter (v. 12).

In the meantime, Titus had plenty to do. He and Paul, as we have seen, had originally been on Crete together, and when Paul moved on, Titus was left behind that he 'might straighten out what was left unfinished' (1.5). In the churches on the island things were not in an entirely satisfactory condition. There were matters that needed to be addressed. And as we have worked our way through Paul's letter we have discovered what those matters were. Elders were to be appointed in every town (1.6-9); there were false teachers to be dealt with (1.10-16); certain things needed to be taught to particular groups of Christians (chapter 2); the church as a whole was to be stirred up to good works (3.3-8)—these were the kinds of things Titus was to be doing during this closing period of his ministry on Crete.

In the passage before us now we have Paul's final instructions. They basically concern two types of men—men who were a *trouble* to the church and men who were a *blessing* to the church.

Men who were a trouble to the church

There were men in the Cretan churches who were doing harm to the believers by the things they were teaching. Paul has already addressed himself to the problem in chapter 1.10-16. Here at the close of his letter he returns to it.

It is difficult to be entirely sure of what these troublemakers were actually saying. In verse 9 Paul refers to 'foolish controversies and genealogies and arguments and quarrels about the law'. In chapter 1:14 mention is also made of 'Jewish myths'. It would seem that the false teachers were Jews who in their teaching were majoring on fanciful stories about Jewish ancestors whose names appear in the genealogies of the Old Testament. They also had plenty to say about Old Testament law and, though the apostle gives us no details, it is clear that they were astray in their interpretation and application of it.

Furthermore, it seems that it was in an atmosphere of argument and quarrels that they were airing their peculiar views. They were possibly fighting among themselves—disputing with one another over the details of their fanciful teaching. It is possible, too, that their disputing was spreading among those members of the church whom the troublemakers had impacted and who had begun to embrace their teaching.

Here were men who were without question a trouble to the church. In verses 9-11 Paul gives Titus some important instruction on how he is to respond to them.

Avoid imitating them

Titus is to 'avoid' these 'foolish controversies and genealogies and arguments and quarrels about the law' (v. 9). He is not to imitate the troublemakers by allowing himself to get drawn into these matters and give his time and strength to them. He is to shun them. Why? Because they are 'unprofitable and useless' (v. 9). It would not be to the spiritual benefit of the Lord's people for their leader and teacher to be taken up with such things. Titus needs to stick to what is profitable. He must major on 'what is in accord with sound doctrine' (2:1).

Contemporary application of this has its challenges. There is an obscurity hanging over the details of what Titus was encountering that makes it difficult to be sure we are comparing like with like as we try to apply Paul's counsel to contemporary situations in the church.

There is, however, one very straightforward application that may be made. In his second letter to Timothy Paul says that 'All Scripture is God-breathed and is useful for teaching, rebuking, correcting and training in righteousness, so that the man of God may be thoroughly equipped for every good work' (2 Tim. 3:16, 17). Notice the word 'useful'. Other translations render it 'profitable'. The controversies of the false teachers were 'unprofitable and useless'. Scripture by contrast is 'profitable'.

> There is a lesson of vital importance here for preachers. What our congregations need and what they always ought to receive is preaching that is profitable to them i.e. preaching that instructs, rebukes, corrects, and trains in righteousness; that equips for Christian service.

There is a lesson of vital importance here for preachers. What our congregations need and what they always ought to receive is preaching that is *profitable* to them i.e. preaching that instructs, rebukes, corrects, and trains in righteousness; that equips for Christian service. There is only one way in which that can be done and that is by giving them preaching that is thoroughly and pervasively *scriptural*. It must be our continual aim to set before our people the teaching of the word of *God*. Only then will we be spiritually useful to them.

Deal decisively with them

In chapter 1 Paul says about the false teachers, 'They must be silenced, because they are ruining whole households' (v. 11).

They were not to be permitted to go on peddling their false teaching unchallenged. Now in chapter 3 a similar note is struck: 'Warn a divisive person once, and then warn him a second time. After that have nothing to do with him. You may be sure that such a man is warped and sinful; he is self-condemned' (vv. 10, 11).

Paul calls the troublemaker 'a divisive person', and in the light of verse 9 it is hardly surprising that he should. Since his teaching was resulting in foolish controversies, arguments, and quarrels he was clearly having a divisive influence in the church. It has happened again and again. Here is a congregation that has gone happily and unitedly along for many years. Then there is a division. And it is not because Mrs. A. has fallen out with the elders, or because Mr. B. has been criticizing the deacons, or because Miss C. is unhappy about the church flowers. It is because someone has introduced error into the church. For though many have recognized it as error and rejected it, others have embraced it as the truth. And the result is a sad *division*.

What then is to be done with such a divisive person? He is first of all to be warned. Titus (presumably in conjunction with the elders) is to speak to him about the divisive course of action he is pursuing, and *warn* him. Church leaders must do exactly the same today. False teaching is too dangerous a thing to be ignored. A divisive person is to be prohibited from teaching his errors anymore. He is to be told to stop disrupting the assembly with his foolish controversies. And if he pays heed, then all is well. The matter need go no further.

If, however, he doesn't heed this first warning, he is to receive a second one. The elders must not shrink back from confronting the man again and repeating what they said before. And if he still will not give heed, Paul's instruction is to 'have nothing to do with him'. Such a person is 'warped and sinful' (v. 11). The church is to dissociate itself from him so that he will no longer be at liberty to pursue his divisive course. His membership is to be severed and there is to be no re-admission until he gives clear evidence of repentance.

Men who were a blessing to the church

Paul writes, verse 13, 'Do everything you can to help Zenas the lawyer and Apollos on their way and see that they have everything they need.' It may well be that Zenas and Apollos were the bearers of this letter. They were going to pass through Crete, deliver the letter, and then move on somewhere else.

Of Zenas we know nothing more than what is recorded here. He is not mentioned anywhere else in the New Testament. Of Apollos, by contrast, we are told a number of different things. Luke informs us in Acts 18, for example, that he was a learned man with a thorough knowledge of the Scriptures. In Ephesus that godly couple, Priscilla and Aquila, were a great help to him for they invited him to their home and there explained the way of God to him more adequately. Later, in Achaia, Apollos was in turn 'a great help to those who by grace had believed. For he vigorously refuted the Jews in public debate, proving from the Scriptures that Jesus was the Christ' (Acts 18:27, 28). On the very safe assumption that Zenas was a fine Christian too, we see whom these instructions concern: men who were a *blessing* to the church.

Meeting their needs

Titus was to do everything he could to help them on their journey. When the New Testament speaks elsewhere about doing this (e.g. Acts 15:3; Rom. 15: 24; 1 Cor. 16:6, 11; 2 Cor. 1:16; 3 John 6-8) the reference is to those who are engaging in some form of Christian ministry. It was very likely the same with Zenas and Apollos. Perhaps they were on a missionary journey, travelling from place to place, teaching and preaching the gospel. Titus was to see that as they moved on from Crete, they had everything they needed.

What that meant in practical terms we can easily guess. They would need food for the journey. Perhaps they would need money as well and maybe some new sandals and a staff, or a fresh change of clothes. Titus was to ensure that they received them.

Involving the church

Paul adds in verse 14, 'Our people must learn to devote themselves to doing what is good, in order that they may provide for daily necessities and not live unproductive lives.' The inclusion of the word 'daily' is somewhat misleading for it gives the impression that the necessities in question were their own necessities—their basic everyday needs. It is much more likely, however, that Paul is referring not to the Cretans' needs but to the needs of men like Zenas and Apollos. Hence William Hendriksen's translation: 'let our people learn to apply themselves to noble deeds for these occasions of imperative need'[1].

This ministry of providing and helping, then, is not just for

Titus. It is one in which the congregation as a whole is to engage. When there is an opportunity like this to assist fellow believers who are in engaging in the work of Christ, they are to consider it their duty and privilege to assist them. It is to be a part of the church's ministry.

Applying it today

It may not be all that common for Christian workers to visit our congregations who require to be helped on their journey in the way that Zenas and Apollos did. Nevertheless it is our privilege from time to time to receive visits from Christian workers. They may be overseas missionaries, or they may be representatives of some Christian organisation.

Paul's words to Titus have their application to such visits. It is the duty and privilege of congregations who receive them to give their visitors practical help. It may be hospitality while they are with us, a monetary gift when they leave, a commitment to send food, or clothes, or Christian books if they are needed—or additional workers! It is in just such practical ways that we ensure that we do not live unproductive lives but rather help to advance the kingdom of God.

> It is the duty and privilege of congregations who receive them to give their visitors practical help. It may be hospitality while they are with us, a monetary gift when they leave, a commitment to send food, or clothes, or Christian books if they are needed—or additional workers!

We may think about it in terms of different callings in life. We may not have been called by God to serve where these visiting believers have been called to serve. By virtue of their calling they have had to leave their native country, perhaps, and live in a very different part of the world. By contrast, we may have been called to remain at home. But we are all part of the same worldwide church and involved in the same worldwide mission to advance our Saviour's cause. And when we support our brethren in practical ways by helping to meet their necessities, we are giving tangible expression to that reality. We are playing our part—along with them—in the fulfilment of the Great Commission and thereby ensuring that we do not live unproductive lives.

Grace—again

The letter ends with greetings and a benediction: 'Everyone with me sends you greetings. Greet those who love us in the faith. Grace be with you all' (v. 15). It is striking that Paul ends here as he began. In his opening greeting he wished for Titus 'grace and peace from God the Father and Christ Jesus our Saviour' (1:4). Now in his farewell he wishes grace again—this time to all the believers as well. How much they needed it! If the outstanding matters in Crete were to be addressed, the difficult situations dealt with, the truths of this letter taught, taken to heart, and lived out in their lives, they greatly needed the grace of God. And for much else besides! Knowing that, Paul makes it his prayerful wish for them: 'Grace be with you all'.

Is our need any less? Not a bit! If we are to take to heart and live out in our lives all that this letter requires us to believe and do we are in as great need of God's grace as the believers in Crete. What a delightful thought that it is available in the same quantities and possesses the same intrinsic power that it did two thousand years ago. May that grace be with us all!

FOR FURTHER STUDY

1 The issue of church discipline is taken up by Paul in other letters, most fully in 1 Corinthians 5 and 2 Thessalonians 3. Read these passages and think about the application of them to situations in the church today. Why is church discipline necessary at times? Why must the church not shrink back from it when it *is* necessary?

2 Follow up the references to helping God's servants on their journey. What range of ministries do you discern in them? What are some of the contemporary parallels to them?

TO THINK ABOUT AND DISCUSS

1. It was noted that contemporary applications of the problem of foolish controversies etc. has its challenges. Can you think, however, of situations past or present that do have parallels to this problem and to which Paul's counsel to Titus applies?

2. What kind of things should preachers either avoid or do in order to ensure that their preaching is in the highest sense useful to their congregations?

3. 'To deal with divisive persons as Paul directs is harsh and unkind.' How would you respond to a person who made that objection?

4. How are we to distinguish between differences of opinion over doctrines which Christians may honestly hold without it being necessary to break fellowship with one another and the kind of error that damages an assembly and requires church discipline?

5. Think about the missionaries and other Christian workers who visit your church. How can you best help them as they continue to serve the Lord?

Endnotes

Chapter 2—Profile of a Christian Leader

1 John R.W. Stott, *The Message of 1 Timothy & Titus*, Inter-Varsity Press, 1996, p.175
2 John Benton, *Straightening out the Self-Centred Church,* Evangelical Press, 1997, p.51

Chapter 3—Dealing with False Teachers

1 William Hendriksen, *New Testament Commentary on 1 & 2 Timothy and Titus,* Banner of Truth Trust, 1976, p.351
2 John R.W. Stott, op cit, pp.183-184

Chapter 4—Teaching for Men

1 William Hendriksen, *op cit*, p.363
2 John Benton, *op cit*, p.79
3 John Benton, *op cit*, p.79
4 John R.W. Stott, *op cit*, p.190

Chapter 5—Teaching for Women

1 William Hendriksen, *op cit*, p.366
Chapter 6—Words for Workers

1 John Stott, op cit, p.143
2 John Murray, Principles of Conduct, Tyndale Press, 1957, p.104

Chapter 7—Living in the Light of His Coming

1 JM Boice, *Expositional Commentary on Romans, Vol.III*, Baker, 1995, p.1036

Chapter 8—The Christian in the World

1 John R.W. Stott, *op cit*, p.199
2 William Hendriksen, *op cit*, p.386
3 Patrick Fairbairn, *The Pastoral Epistles*, T&T Clark, 1874, p.289

Chapter 9—God's Saving Work

1 John Murray, *Collected Writings, Vol.2*, Banner of Truth Trust, 1977, p.170

Chapter 10—Final Instructions

1 William Hendriksen, *op cit*, p.399

Additional Resources

John Benton, *Straightening out the Self-Centred Church* (Welwyn Commentary Series): Evangelical Press

Patrick Fairbairn, *The Pastoral Epistles*: T&T Clark

Gordon D. Fee, *1 and 2 Timothy, Titus* (New International Biblical Commentary): Hendrickson

William Hendriksen, *New Testament Commentary on 1 & 2 Timothy and Titus*: Banner of Truth Trust

George W. Knight, *The Pastoral Epistles* (The New International Greek Testament Commentary): Eerdmans, Paternoster

William D. Mounce, *Pastoral Epistles* (Word Biblical Commentary): Thomas Nelson

John R.W. Stott, *The Message of 1 Timothy & Titus* (The Bible Speaks Today): Inter-Varsity Press

OPENING UP TITUS